By Word of Mouth

POEMS FROM THE SPANISH
1916–1959

aprile 16, 1941   ①

PORTO RICO TALK

1. A statement as to the modern
basis of poetic form (informal)

2. Read some illustrative verses

3. Spanish (Portugese) and
American-English. Our profitable
interrelationship in developing
a new poetic form : EXAMPLE -
Lope de Vega vs Shakespeare as
a model (form) for America :
What we might profit etc etc

****

Preamble

The difficulty is to keep such
a talk as this informal.

After all, there is no great
point at issue. We are here for
the most part to look at each
other, to recognize in each
other - that curious complexity
called a writer, to encourage
and to learn. But most to try to
find a means, through the art
which we practise, to communicat
with each other - for what may
come of it.

WCW's notes for his talk at the
First Inter-American Writers' Conference
of the University of Puerto Rico
(Beinecke Rare Book and Manuscript Library)

William Carlos Williams

By Word of Mouth

POEMS FROM THE SPANISH
1916–1959

COMPILED AND EDITED BY **JONATHAN COHEN**
FOREWORD BY **JULIO MARZÁN**

A NEW DIRECTIONS BOOK

Acknowledgments are due to the editors of the following journals and websites
   where some of these translations have appeared: *The Hudson Review*, *The New
   Yorker*, *Translation Review*, and *Words Without Borders*.

Book design by Sylvia Frezzolini Severance
Manufactured in the United States of America
New Directions Books are printed on acid-free paper
First published as a New Directions Paperbook Original (NDP1210) in 2011.
Published simultaneously in Canada by Penguin Books Canada Limited

Library of Congress Cataloging-in-Publication Data

By word of mouth : poems from the Spanish, 1916-1959 / [translated by William
Carlos Williams]; compiled and edited by Jonathan Cohen ; foreword by Julio
Marzán.
p. cm.
A bilingual collection of William Carlos Williams' translations of various Spanish
and Latin American poets.
Includes bibliographical references and index.
ISBN 978-0-8112-1885-6 (paperbook : alk. paper)
1. Spanish poetry—20th century—Translations into English. 2. Spanish poetry—
20th century. 3. Spanish American poetry—20th century—Translations into Eng-
lish. 4. Spanish American poetry—20th century. I. Williams, William Carlos, 1883-
1963. II. Cohen, Jonathan, 1949 May 4–
PQ6187.B9 2011
861'.608—dc23

                              2011023576

10 9 8 7 6 5 4 3 2 1

New Directions Books are published for James Laughlin
by New Directions Publishing Corporation
80 Eighth Avenue, New York 10011

Contents

Sweated Blood / 1940s & '50s

Foreword:
William Carlos Williams, Translator

William Carlos Williams's "The Desert Music" opens with his crossing a bridge into Mexico and coming upon "a form / propped motionless." It is "Egg-shaped!" and evokes the Old West's stereotype of the siesta-time Mexican, on his haunches and covered in a serape ("knees hugged tight into the belly / . . . What a place to sleep!"). Being exactly midway on the bridge makes it "interjurisdictional, not to be disturbed," the same metaphysical plane of poetry on which Williams articulates an ars poetica that is by now well known: "Say it, no ideas but in things." Less known is the baroque imagination interwoven into "The Desert Music," providing for an autobiographical reading based on cultural contrast and identity.

Williams recounts his visit to the Mexican border city in the voice of two personae. Bill is impatient with the Mexican imagery, and Carlos is more receptive. On crossing back into the United States, Williams contemplates the form again, this time called to it by the titular "desert music." The music surrounds the form, like an embryonic sack, defining it, already a visible symbol of poetry, but now also a metaphor of Williams's rebirth of consciousness after his inner conflict experienced in Mexico. Like the desert, the poem spans cultures. Like the desert music, the form's music is also "interjurisdictional." Williams, in the line of the two cultures connected by the bridge, is midway and, as a poet, "interjurisdictional." Seeing this stasis in the sleeping form reminds him that he is foremost an artist: "I *am* a poet! I / am. I am. I am a poet."

The border imagery of "The Desert Music" is not insignificant, of course: to understand Williams as a poet, one must appreciate the role of translation in both his life and work. He was the son of Elena Hoheb Williams, whose first language was Spanish. She had studied painting in Paris and was his lifelong muse. Traceable to her influence, despite her conservative taste in art, Williams's poetry emulates painting. Williams needed to reconcile his decided Americanness and the culture's proclivity to dismiss his Hispanic background. His writings can be read as a consciously elaborated Cubist self-portrait that allowed the coexistence of these conflicting cultural perspectives.

Williams worked out this conflict not in any social or political or ethnic discourse that we might expect today but in his art. Unfortunately, his stylistic "scheme" went over the head of an established aesthetic convention that distinguished literary art from themes and writings deemed marginal to mainstream American culture. His "scheme" allowed him to artistically encode the challenges he faced in metaphor while preserving his authority as a mainstream poet, focused on the business of the poem. The ambiguity of this "scheme" enabled the critics to be selective and read Williams as perpetuating a traditional cultural agenda.

Consequently, Williams's passion for modernism in art is widely discussed but not his desire to fracture rigid traditions that subverted what he believed to be the true American spirit; these traditions denied other than Anglo-Protestant cultural tributaries, among them his Hispanic lineage. Starting out ambivalent about diverting from the mainstream, he wrote, in "At Kenneth Burke's Place," of joining with fellow poets who spoke of "hating" the marginal, cited in the poem as the "'Esoteric'" and "the colored," which are "not to be included in our anthologies." He ultimately not only accepted but advocated the marginality of his mother's ancestry, both as a fount of artistic novelty and as the true origin of his American identity. He acquired even more confidence in his interpretation of Americanness by rereading American history (*In the American Grain*) and from the art emerging in Europe—Hispanic culture had produced Pablo Picasso and had produced him.

Unfortunately, the American literary consciousness that ascribed prestige to certain foreign cultures did not extend such prestige to Anglo culture's historical rival since Henry VIII, demoting even further its domestic manifestations. Predictably, therefore, Ezra Pound jibed that Williams was a "foreigner," advising that he would do better to identify with his English-born father. Pound, who started out studying Spanish literature (which he subsequently called "Dago Lit") and never finished his dissertation on Spanish baroque poetry, later brushed aside Hispanic literature and culture as of "just savages," as he wrote to Williams.

Savage as applied to the Spanish has a long Anglo-Saxon history. Pound's English ancestors, in their propaganda against Spain, used *savage* frequently to characterize Spain's conquistadors as brutal and to depict their having sex with the Indians as bestiality. Notably, as Williams reads the history of the Americas, it was that physical intercourse with the natives that gave birth to the real American spirit. The Spanish, as he interpreted in *In the American Grain*, came to baptize and "touch" the natives and, consequently, arrived prepared to consume and be consumed by America. That included rape but also marriage. As a consequence, for all its evils, the Spanish conquest produced something "greater than the gold" they extracted, what Williams called "the mingling." In contrast, the "squeamish" Puritans came neither to touch nor be touched by American nature or its natives, and therefore had "nothing to do with America."

Williams could boast of inheriting the truest American spirit because his family was the product of that "mingling," having come from where it first occurred, the Caribbean. His father, William George, was taken at the age of five from England to the Dominican Republic. His mother, Elena, was born on the then-Spanish colony Puerto Rico, descending from a lineage that went back to other Afro-Caribbean isles and further back to the Sephardic Jewish Dutch. She also spoke fluent French. Additionally, both his parents and his English grandmother practiced spiritualism—a Romantic-age French affectation throughout Latin America—and thus enhanced Williams's appreciation of the commingling of the spiritual and physical worlds. (That emphasis on spirit would link Williams to the transcendentalists, and to Whitman, who also, untraditionally, looked upon Spain as "maternal.")

Pound's disdain of Elena's background was viewed by Williams as symptomatic of this culture's not understanding the spiritual heritage that made it American. Pound failed to understand that Williams identified himself as American *because* of his Hispanic background. Pound harbored the resistant ethnocentrism that constituted Williams's core challenge as artist, what he called his particular artist's "weather"—the antagonistic forces that in every era energize artists. Williams, in other words, confronted a definition of American culture contradicted by the country's reality. He was forced to reconcile being the poet Bill in public, as Pound advised, while in fact he was both Bill and Carlos to himself.

This inner drama also kept him cognizant of being like a river with many tributaries. In defiance of his "weather," he wrote intending to be a turbulent voice of newness against a tradition-hardened America. Where Pound's mythos erected an ethnocentric barricade, a mental Plymouth Plantation that excluded him, Williams was convinced that he embodied the purer idea of America. In affirming this Americanness, Williams treated as equivalent his advocacy of modernism in art, his own poetry and prose, and his celebration of a legacy in the Spanish language.

For if English and Spanish competed in the mainstream mythos, Williams grew up inspired by both: by books in both languages in the family library, by William George's Spanish fluency and literacy, and Elena's spoken Spanish, her accented English, and her mixture of both, along with French. To the poetry of his mother's struggle to communicate, Williams devoted the book *Yes, Mrs. Williams*, consisting of vignettes in which he celebrated growing up understanding language to be a translation of an essential music. That book is also a tacit ars poetica, informing us that underlying his amply articulated tenets on poetry is the principle of translation. Whether making poems of life experiences or marveling at the semantic possibilities in Elena's mispronunciations and malapropisms, he was translating ambient aesthetic essence into artistic form.

Spanish, in other words, was functional in the Williams household and not just ceremonial; even though Williams wrote in English and spoke a poor Spanish, he saw himself and his work as descending literally from his Spanish legacy, his—always in quotation marks—"line." That "line" is genealogical through Elena, but is also the poetic line that Williams favored in answer to the iambic, the Spanish eight-syllable line that he traced back to the seventeenth-century baroque poets Francisco Quevedo and especially Luis de

Góngora, whose experimentation with words and ambiguity Picasso credited as the origin of Cubism. Williams even advocated that American poets should count syllables and not the traditional meters. His verse play *Tituba's Children* is written in eight-syllable lines, and in every poem with baroque touches he renders tribute to his "line."

Poets of that "line" appear to be the "sources" that Williams claims none will know to identify. ("But they have no access to my sources.") That "line,"however, was largely inspirational, invisible until Williams cast light on it, as he did in his poetry or prose. "Hymn to Love Ended" is one such poem, subtitled "Imaginary Translation from the Spanish," although, except for the title's baroque-style pun, the poem has nothing ostensible to do with Spanish. Another homage to his baroque lineage and, of course, implicitly what he coined an "imaginary translation," is the poem "El Hombre." The title is a tribute to Góngora, whom Williams in an essay called "the man!"

"El Hombre" is well known as the subject of Wallace Stevens's "Nuances on a Theme by Williams." Notwithstanding Stevens's metaphysical reading, on another semantic level "El Hombre," an exercise in baroque wordplay, is also autobiographical. Consider its first couplet, "It is a strange courage / you give me ancient star." This "strange courage" derives from a "foreign heart." The second line refers to Hélène, "bright light" or "star," and uses "ancient" as an alternate for "old." Old Elena did give him a foreign heart.

"El Hombre" is also an imitation of Góngora and Quevedo, this being one way Williams could render tribute to his "tributaries." In the opening pages of the first book of *Paterson*, a stanza imitates the rhythm of a hallmark stanza in a poem by Luis Palés Matos, in whom he identified resonances of his own work. Palés Matos's *Tuntún de pasa y grifería: poemas afroantillanos* ("Tom-Tom of Kinky Hair and Things Black: Afro-Antillean Poems") paralleled Williams's use of popular diction and being informed by tributaries from the past, by lingering spirits of place (Palés Matos's was a white *criollo* infused with the Caribbean's mingling of African and Hispanic cultures). Not by coincidence, the year that Williams said he came upon a "scheme" for *Paterson* was the year that he traveled to Puerto Rico and received Palés Matos's book—which also not uncoincidentally descends from Góngora.

Like imitation, translating from the Spanish was another way Williams honored his "tributaries," which is not to portray Williams as an activist translator—although in some cases one could call him that—as many of the poems that he translated were recommended by others, particularly Professor Vázquez-Amaral of Rutgers, who had been referred to the New Jersey poet by Pound. Nevertheless, from Williams's own observations, we see he took on those commissions as continuations of his poetry writing, opportunities to write another poem. More important, it would appear from the translations that, whether the poem was suggested by others or taken on by Williams himself, the final result evinced its emerging from an intersection of his life or work and his "line"; the translations resonated with his own voice. These translations, therefore, are best read not just as a means to discovering great poetry in Spanish; they are also portals to understanding Williams as poet.

That Williams approached translation as more than a linguistic or literary exercise possibly explains why, from the poets from Spain, there are notable absences. For instance, Williams wrote on, but didn't finally translate, the most famous Spanish poet of his era, Federico García

Lorca. Perhaps because García Lorca had already been translated, but one can also infer that Williams, while admiring Lorca, did not specifically identify himself in Lorca's work. Instead, among the poets of the Spanish Civil War, Williams translated lesser known and anonymous poets with whose voices he identified and politically sympathized; the poets from Spain also responded to a widely shared sympathy for the cause of the Spanish Republic.

Also notably absent from Spain's poets are his two major influences, Quevedo and especially Góngora (though he did translate, with his mother, what he thought was Quevedo's novella, *The Dog and the Fever*,* plus a couple of fragments of his poetry). One can deduce that Williams demurred from attempting to translate the impossible density of these two poets, although one can consider his "imaginary translations" as his way of interpreting their influence in his own poetry.

Finally, about Spain one can extrapolate that even though Williams did identify with Hispanic culture as the origin of his "line" and identified its tributary "mingling" spirit, Spain itself is distant to his consciousness. More tangible autobiographical and literary connections are evident in the poems from Latin America. For example, in his translation of "Three Nahuatl Poems" (or, more accurately, from the Spanish translations of the Nahuatl original), we come upon lines evocative of Williams's consciousness: "Where am I to go, whither? / The road's there, the road to Two-Gods" and "He has fled to the place where all lack a body."

---

* *The Dog and the Fever*, long attributed to Quevedo, is now thought by virtually all scholars of early modern Spanish literature to be the work of Pedro de Espinosa, a contemporary of his, who also was a poet and prose writer. Williams's book acknowledges the question of authorship, yet repeats the old belief that Quevedo published the novella under Espinosa's name. —JC

That last image, evoking spiritualism, is consistent with his having translated poems by Rafael Arévalo Martínez and José Asunción Silva, both fin-de-siècle romantic poets strongly influenced by spiritualism. Arévalo Martínez was a particular favorite of William George, with whom Williams translated Arévalo Martínez's short story "The Man Who Resembled a Horse." Translations, often with the linguistic assistance of his Spanish-fluent father, show that his English father was the Spanish authority in the household (contradicting the simplistic allegory that he represented the Anglo cultural influence on Williams), and that translation was an important ceremony of cultural influence in Williams's bicultural life.

Beyond family spiritualist sensibilities that would attract him to poems by Arévalo Martínez, Williams must have also read in the following lines an image of himself as translator: "When I met her I loved myself. / It was she who had my best singings." A similar mirror-like appeal seems evident in Asunción Silva's "The Disease of the Century," a patient-doctor dialogue on the poet's disillusion with his time.

Autobiographical resonances are even more evident in Williams's translations of his Latin American contemporaries. In José Santos Chocano's "The Song of the Road," the central music image parallels that of "The Desert Music." The speaker's caring for his aged mother in Alfonso Guillén Zelaya's "Lord, I Ask a Garden" evokes Williams caring for his mother. Similarly, Eugenio Florit's "Conversation with My Father" images Williams's relationship with his father. Williams translated Palés Matos's "Prelude in Boricua," identifying with his being from his mother's island and the poem's use of colloquial speech—"Boricua" here not meaning the place but the popular speech of

Puerto Rico. Translations of Neruda, Paz, and Parra generally mark an artistic kinship in modernism, while Williams surely saw dimensions of his own imagination in Neruda's surrealism and in Parra's "anti-poetic" monologues, although he was surely again attracted, in "Piano Solo," to the séance in the lines describing a soul who wants "to find its proper body."

In the epigraph that Jonathan Cohen chose for this book, Williams states that his translations fit into a "scheme," suggesting that they reiterate the discourse of his poetry when, strictly speaking, they do not. His own poems offer themselves as paradigms of Imagism and concreteness, shunning abstraction and sentiment. His Bill persona criticizes his mother for drowning in her nostalgia for Paris and San Juan. In "The Desert Music," Bill mocks the romantic sentimentality of Mexican music.

In contrast, Williams translated poems that we wouldn't readily associate with the poet, poems that interpret the *corazón* (although he wrote of Kora in her hell zone), poems steeped in spirit or that capture metaphysical moments, such as Paz's "Hymn Among the Ruins" and Ocampo's "The Infinite Horses." These translations do not extend the surface discourse of Williams's poetry but fit into his composite "scheme," which, as noted at the opening of this foreword, was the composing of a Cubist self-portrait of his conflicting cultural personae.

To illustrate, Williams as Bill promoted the English stereotype of Spanish, juxtaposing English as the more rational and concrete language beside Spanish as evocative of Latinate ideation, sentimentality, and romance. The Anglo-American "Bill" is the poet whom the critics embraced, overlooking that, throughout his work, Williams explicitly called attention to an alternate Carlos voice, more often subtextual, as in "El Hombre," revealing the condition of Williams's "foreign heart." In the translations, Carlos rises to the surface to speak of intangibles. In this way the translations fit into the "scheme" of stasis, his two cultures bridged. They are another celebration of his Carlos lineage, transmitting to this culture its "mingling" spirit—Bill tensely fused with Carlos is Williams the American poet.

Williams defines a true American as a sower, "mingling"—not Pound's notion—like the personages of *In the American Grain* and the artists and poets, past and present, whom he collected to be part of his "band," an American *conjunto* in his spiritual "line." In his poem "Tribute to Neruda the Poet Collector of Seashells" (Williams himself was a collector), he appeals to the deceased Elena—she never cared for her son's modern poems—not to be as critical of Neruda as she had been of him: "Be patient with / him, darling mother." In the poem, Neruda becomes Elena's adopted son. Presumably, her brood includes the poets translated here.

JULIO MARZÁN
New York, 2011

Introduction:
Into the American Idiom—
Poems from the Spanish

Tain't what a man sez, but wot he means
that the traducer has got to bring over. —Ezra Pound

Rigor of beauty is the quest. —William Carlos Williams

This book is the first compilation of William Carlos Williams's translations of Spanish and Latin American poetry that he made during the course of his literary career, starting in the decade of the First World War, and continuing through his final years in the late 1950s. The translations here are presented in roughly chronological order, and are organized in keeping with the different periods of his activity translating poems from Spanish. A few rendered in the earlier periods have been omitted because their poetic quality doesn't measure up to that of the rest. The bilingual format is used to allow readers to see what Williams accomplished as a translator, and also to allow the poets he translated to speak for themselves.

Spanish was Williams's first language, but he never really mastered it in terms of native fluency or sophistication. It was the language of his parents' home in Rutherford, New Jersey, where he was born and ultimately spent his entire life. Williams's son Bill Jr., in Neil Baldwin's biography *To All Gentleness*, describes the duality of his father's early years: "The common language in his home when he was a growing boy was Spanish. The family diet, mores, expletives, heroes and manner of dress were anything but American. On the other hand, his familiars in the community, the children of the Hyslops, Alyeas, Browns, Armstrongs and Livingstons were all as American as baked beans and apple pie, natives of this land for generations, not an immigrant in the lot."

The Hispanic otherness of his home against his larger social and cultural world in Rutherford, together with the external forces of assimilation in the air, clearly fueled in him a burning desire to be American and speak American. Indeed, Williams's great achievement as the preeminent U.S. poet of the twentieth century was to create a modern American poetics based on American speech, thought, and experience.

Williams translated poetry not only from Spanish but also from French, in which he was fairly fluent, as well as from Chinese and Greek (for which he was helped by others who knew those languages). His translations from the Spanish were the most personal, given his deep connection with the language. He viewed poetry translation as a critical and creative endeavor. It long attracted him. As he told Nicholas Calas in a letter in 1940 when he was translating Calas's poetry from the French: "It is a *fascinating problem* to try to put [the] *exact meaning* into an *equivalent English*. I enjoy such work." The second letter Williams sent Calas the same day is even more revealing of Williams's attitude toward poetry translation: "All this fits well into my scheme. I don't care how I say what I must say. If I do original work all well and good. But if I can say it (the matter of form I mean) by translating the work of others that also is valuable. What difference does it make?" Translation for him was, above all, an act of poetry.

Williams produced a slim but ample body of verse translations from the Spanish, rendering the work of about thirty different poets (some anonymous). Many of these translations were published in his collections of poetry and in little magazines, while others have until now remained in manuscript form as hidden treasures in library archives. They include magnificent poems that demonstrate the force of his efforts to broaden the scope of American writing by bringing in Spanish-language poetry. He recognized that "a translation into another language involves in the first place a choice of the language into which the translation is to be made" ("Robert Lowell's Verse Translation"). For Williams, this language was not "English," but the language of the "local American way of speaking," which he famously called the American idiom. On this point he was emphatic, as he says in the note to *Sappho*, his folio translation published in 1957: "I don't speak English, but the American idiom. I don't know how to write anything else, and I refuse to learn. . . . I have been as accurate as the meaning of the words permitted—always with a sense of our own American idiom to instruct me." Even in his earliest ventures as a translator, motivated by his friend Ezra Pound, Williams can be seen breaking away from the artificial language of Victorian poetry and using the American language spoken in real life.

That Williams grew up in a Spanish-speaking home clearly influenced his interest in translating Spanish. In his autobiography, in the chapter titled "Translations," he describes his ambition: "I have always wanted to do some translations from the Spanish. It was my mother's native language [she was Puerto Rican] as well as one which my father [English West Indian] spoke from childhood. But more than that the language has a strong appeal for me, temperamentally, as a relief from the classic mood of both French and Italian. Spanish is not, in the sense to which I refer, a literary language. It has a place of its own, an independent place very sympathetic to the New World." Williams elaborates by saying "this independence, this lack of integration with our British past gives us an opportunity, facing Spanish literature [including Latin American], to make new appraisals, especially in attempting translations, which should permit us to use our language with unlimited freshness."

This "freshness" for him was always central to his aspirations as a poet defining the modernist MAKE IT NEW tradition, and Williams approached making verse translations from the Spanish as a way to extend the range and capacity of American poetry. "In such attempts," he explains, "we will not have to follow precedent but can branch off into a new diction, adapting new forms, even discovering new forms in our attempts to find accurate equivalents."

Underlying Williams's efforts to give voice to Spanish and Latin American poets through translation, in addition to his literary and aesthetic ambitions, was his personal mixed ethnicity. His translations here can certainly be viewed as expressions of his Hispanic self. Rod Townley, in his brilliant study *The Early Poetry of William Carlos Williams*, explains well: "Between the two bland William's of his name there lurks a Carlos, a 'dark Spanish beauty,' as [Penn's] 1906 Medical School yearbook, *The 'Scope*, called Williams." Although later in his life he could publicly say he was "half-Spanish" (*I Wanted to Write a Poem*), he wasn't always so open about that (or about his Jewish roots). He knew well the prevailing American attitude toward "furriners" and immigrant people with even slightly dark skin like himself, whether from Spain or Latin

America. He saw clearly the racial bigotry behind it; he understood he needed to cover the Spanish part of his ethnic identity in certain public situations—to fit in to succeed. For instance, in a 1941 letter, he was careful in providing biographical details to Louis Untermeyer for the note to appear in Untermeyer's forthcoming anthology of American poetry: "Not much Spanish in me despite my middle name."

Concerning the translation poetics that Williams applied to his work, successful translation for him, in general, meant a faithful "paraphrase" of the other language, as defined long ago by Dryden: "translation with latitude, where the author is kept in view by the translator, so as never to be lost, but his words are not so strictly followed as his sense; and that too is admitted to be amplified, but not altered." Williams usually translated line by line, and in the sense-for-sense manner, often working with a prosaic literal translation provided by someone else. Occasionally, however, in a line here and there he did alter the sense, but not the verbal texture and tone. For example, in the third section of Jorge Carrera Andrade's "Dictated by the Water," he rendered the line "mayúscula inicial de la blancura" as "start with a blank anesthesia," which seems all the more curious in light of the literal translation, "initial capital of whiteness," though equally enigmatic, which he had on his desk along with the Spanish.

Ultimately, his translations are never fully in the mode of "imitation," in which the translator—again, to quote Dryden—"assumes the liberty, not only to vary words and sense, but to forsake them both as he sees occasion; and taking only some general hints from the original, to run division on the groundwork, as he pleases." Williams generally didn't go that far, as, for instance, Pound did in his

"Homage to Sextus Propertius" and Lowell did in his *Imitations*. That said, his rendering of Eunice Odio's homage to him, "Al poeta William Carlos Williams" ("To W.C.W."), is an exception, and certainly must be read as an imitation.

In these translations, as Williams did increasingly with his own poetry over time, he explored the use of real speech with its distinctive rhythms and colorations. He aimed for lines that offered poetic equivalence (always an approximation at best) in the American idiom—the way English is spoken in America, what he deemed "one of the greatest of modern languages waiting only for a genius of its intrinsic poetry to appear," as he told the young Harold Norse, whose poetry and verse translations he encouraged. Beyond the literal meaning of words, Williams wanted to instill the language of his translations with the character of "American," which he defined (for Norse) in terms of its measure: "It is in the measure of our speech, in its prosody, that our idiom is distinctive." He wanted to make translations that were living poems whose lines used cadences true to real speech; that is, the spoken measure and the intonational phrasing of the American idiom.

In making these poems from the Spanish, Williams worked at giving the voice of each poet he translated—including the sixteenth-century Spanish poet Lupercio de Argensola and the anonymous Aztec poets—the music of American speech. He worked at re-creating the individual poems' tonal shifts and movement. And above all, with his maturity as a poet, he aimed to produce poems of the same poetic excellence as the authors' verse, to convey the implications of their words, and to use language charged with real feeling.

The translations in this section originally appeared in the August 1916 issue of *Others* (1915–1919), of which Williams was an associate editor at the time—and in this issue, probably the main force. The previous year he had started corresponding with the magazine's principal editor, Alfred Kreymborg, with whom he quickly developed a close friendship. This led to his active involvement with the group of avant-garde poets—Wallace Stevens, Maxwell Bodenheim, Marianne Moore, Mina Loy, to name a few—associated with Kreymborg and the "gang" at the summer artists' colony not far from Rutherford, on the New Jersey Palisades. Williams says in his autobiography that *Others* was "the magazine which had saved my life as a writer." It was all about the "new verse" and modernist innovation. And it apparently was the first little magazine in the twentieth century to devote a special issue to Latin American poets in translation.

Called the Spanish-American Number, this issue presented the work of seven poets who were introduced as "some of the most prominent poets among our neighbors of Central and South America." It fit right in with the experimental verse published in the magazine, where, as Williams points out, "it seemed daring to omit capitals at the head of each poetic line" and "rhyme went by the board." The larger context of the Spanish-American Number was the popular interest in the "other" America generated by the Pan American movement at the turn of the last century. This interest peaked around the First World War and the years immediately after it, when translations of Latin American verse flourished, despite the rising tide of wartime nationalism and xenophobia, and the prevalent disdain for Latin American culture among the established arbiters of taste. *Others'* promotion of an inter-American poetry exchange was nothing less than avant-garde.

The authorship of these translations needs to be addressed. In *Others*, they are attributed solely to "W. G. Williams, who is related to our North American friend, William Carlos Williams, as father to son." How, then, can credit be given to the poet son? Based on family history and literary evidence, the most reasonable conclusion is that both can share the credit of authorship, and that these translations are the result of their collaboration. There is no hard documentary evidence of who actually did the lion's share of the work. Their collaboration on the translation of Rafael Arévalo Martínez's 1915 story, "The Man Who Resembled a Horse," made during the same period, points to a similar approach to the authorship of the verse translations here, as does their modernist style, avoiding the use of rhyme and the archaic language associated with Victorian translation poetics.

The first publication of the translation of this story was in *The Little Review* in December 1918 (the month and year his father died), and the attribution is solely to William Carlos Williams. The subsequent publication of the story, in New Directions' 1944 annual anthology, however, has a credit line saying "translated from the Spanish by Wm. Geo. Williams and his son Wm. Carlos Williams." The story there is followed by a note on the translation, written by Carlos Williams, in which he says: "In his last years when [my father] was getting ready to die [of colon cancer] I tried to invent ways to keep him entertained, one of them happened to be to help me translate Rafael Arévalo Martínez's story." Another, surely, was the translation project for *Oth-*

ers. George Williams was very much a traditionalist in his own literary taste, and naturally inclined toward translating poetry in the prevailing Victorian manner, not in the "new verse" manner of Carlos Williams, using colloquial speech without rhyme and abandoning meter for measure. The generous full credit he gave his father, who before he met Pound had been his literary confidante, was done to honor him and cheer him.

Further support for the joint authorship of these translations comes from Williams scholars. Emily Mitchell Wallace, author of *A Bibliography of William Carlos Williams*, explains (personal communication): "As a young scholar I was definitely too cautious in saying 'WCW *probably* assisted his father in translating and in editing the translations for publication in this periodical' [*Bibliography*, entry C11a]. Because WCW was associate editor of this issue of *Others*, he can absolutely be assumed to have assisted his father, as that is what a good editor does, even if the writer is not related. We know, for example, from his correspondence with Wallace Stevens, and others, that he did not hesitate to offer advice whether or not asked to do so. Certainly, his accounts about translating the short story with his father support this common sense conclusion."

Paul Mariani, author of *William Carlos Williams: A New World Naked*, states in this biography: "Since the father was also an impeccable speaker and reader of Spanish, he collaborated with his son (shortly before his death) on a group of translations from the works of several South American writers"—namely, the poets presented in *Others*. Responding to recent queries, he says about the translations (personal communication): "They may be more George Williams's work. Still, I have a strong sense that they really did work together on these." Again, the very method of translation points to the clear and defining hand of the poet son.*

During the period when *Others'* Spanish-American Number came about, Williams was working on the poems that he published the following year in his first mature book of poetry (his third book), the one that showed his distinctive American voice. This book, which uses a Spanish phrase meaning "to him who wants it" for its title, *Al Que Quiere!*, strongly reflects his Hispanic and Puerto Rican roots, and has for an epigraph a passage taken from Arévalo Martínez's story. The epigraph appears only in Spanish and opens this way: "Había sido un arbusto desmedrado que prolonga sus filamentos hasta encontrar el humus necesario en una tierra neuva [*sic*]. Y cómo me nutría!" Or, in his American rendition: "I had been an adventurous shrub which prolongs its filaments until it finds the necessary humus in new earth. And how I fed!"

And Spain Sings / 1930s

The translations in this section are exclusively poems from Spain, mostly *romances*, or ballads, from around the fifteenth century (possibly older) and also from the late 1930s, specifically, the years of the Spanish Civil War (1936–1939) when the old Spanish ballad tradition served as a model for political poems widely embraced by the people of Spain, recited, or sung, at rallies and even in the trenches of the battlefront. "Poplars of the Meadow" harks back to Williams's earliest efforts as a poet and translator, and to the early days

---

*Comparison of the Williams translation of José Santos Chocano's "The Song of the Road" with that made by John Pierrepont Rice demonstrates modernist versus Victorian translation poetics (see Annotations, p. 137).

of his friendship with Pound, who had recommended translation to him as an ideal way to develop technique. In fact, it was Pound who gave Williams the anthology of Spanish poetry where he discovered this anonymous *romance* and others that attracted him. Williams included an earlier, less sophisticated version of it in his second book, *The Tempers* (1913), presenting it with three other *romances* in a group he called "Translations from the Spanish 'El Romancero.'" In his autobiography, he confesses: "I tried to bring over a few when I was just beginning to find myself, but I was not ready for them."

The revised translation of "Poplars of the Meadow" appears in his *Adam & Eve & the City*, published September 1936, just two months after the civil war broke out. Notably gone in the revision is the old-fashioned use of inversions and archaic language: "God, wilt Thou give me patience / Here while suffer I ye" becomes "May God give me patience / Here in my misery." The revision forms part of the new sequence called "Translations from the Spanish," opening with Argensola's "Canción" in both Spanish and English.

The civil war broke Williams's heart and infuriated him, as did the widespread American indifference to the suffering of the Spanish people. He was politically motivated to support the cause of the Republicans (loyalists) fighting Franco. Not only did he translate the three *romances* here written by Spaniards actually fighting in the war, he also made public statements to protest against Franco. For instance, in the activist book, *Writers Take Sides: Letters about the War in Spain from 418 American Authors,* published in 1938 by the League of American Writers, Williams spelled out his position for the public record, as much as for Pound, with whom his long friendship had grown painfully strained over the war: "If Italian history could look down on Mussolini today it would vomit! Think of the century-long struggles for freedom waged by Florence, by Milan, by Venice . . . and then think of the decay of freedom rotting its way into Spain today. . . . Without Mussolini there could not be Franco, it is the same rot eating in. I am for the legal government and the people of Republican Spain."

He did much more than that, too. From mid-1937 until the war's end, he served as chairman of the Bergen County Medical Board to Aid Spanish Democracy. In June, he told his friend Louis Zukofsky that his "few spare moments [were] being taken up" by the work of this medical supplies group. And in July, the day after the first anniversary of the war's outbreak, he wrote to Upton Sinclair to buy twenty copies of his privately printed new novel, *No Pasarán! They Shall Not Pass: A Story of the Siege of Madrid*, to put in his office "for patients to take away." He told Sinclair that "it strengthens conviction in those of us who are already convinced" and that it would compel others to think and, hopefully, sympathize. Even after the war, he continued for several years to contribute to survivors of the Abraham Lincoln Brigade.

Not surprisingly, in view of his political position, Williams was very receptive to the invitation to contribute to M. J. Benardete and Rolfe Humphries's collaborative effort to publish a collection of translations of civil war ballads, "for the American public in sympathy with the Spanish Democracy." Their source for these ballads was the weekly paper published in Madrid, *El mono azul*, which Rafael Alberti among others edited; its name plays on the double meaning of the Spanish, that is, blue coverall, the uniform worn by loyalist fighters, and blue monkey. The translation project, with the support of the League of American Writers, took place in early 1937, and resulted in the book called *And Spain Sings: Fifty Loyalist Ballads Adapted by American Poets*. It came out later that year. Here, Williams published the first English translation of Miguel Hernández, plus the work of two lesser-known poets who quickly faded into obscurity (though it has been conjectured one might be Alberti using a pseudonym).

Humphries, a young academic and poet who was well connected with the New York literati, commissioned all the writers: Stanley Kunitz, Katherine Ann Porter, Edna St. Vincent Millay, Muriel Rukeyser, Shaemas O'Sheel, in addition to Williams and others. Humphries himself did a lot of translations in the book. He sent each poet the Spanish original with a literal version made by Benardete, a Spanish professor. "The call," he explained in his foreword, "was for poets willing to turn literal but rhythmical prose—'rough translations' is too modest a term—into English metrical forms." All the poets were "asked to come as close as they could to the Spanish letter and spirit both." Given the rush to print, he acknowledged the element of haste in the translation process and the effort "to make up for literal exactness by poetic telepathy."

Williams's contributions to this well-received engagé book certainly achieved the vibrant poetic quality expected of him, despite the few lapses in literal fidelity. Of course, his work is not "metrical" in the conventional sense, but follows the spoken measure of the American idiom. His translations also create their own verbal music and rhythms in free verse that, out of necessity, departs from the traditional Spanish ballad form with its eight-syllable line and pattern of rhyming vowels, which sound natural to the Spanish ear, but not in American poetry.

In the fall of 1938, Williams watched as the Republican government was losing the war. Its final campaign was undermined by the Franco-British appeasement of Hitler in Munich with the concession of Czechoslovakia, which effectively destroyed Republican morale by ending hope of an anti-fascist alliance with Western powers. Williams felt crushed. He further immersed himself in the tradition of Spanish poetry, for the comfort it could offer him now and for the light it shed on his own poetry, specifically, the reason why the great Spanish poetry endured and lived beyond its time. It was then that he set about to write his progressive essay on Federico García Lorca to study the sources of his poetic power, which he deemed "are at the beginnings of Spanish literature."

Lorca, who was murdered by the fascists at the start of the war, was in Williams's eyes the greatest poet of modern Spain. In his autobiography, he describes his interest in translating him: "The chief challenge to us today is Lorca and through him Góngora. . . . [P]utting them over into our language, we have almost an ideal opportunity for trying out new modes entirely separate from anything either English or French. I must confess I have done nothing yet to carry this work on, but it strongly attracts me and someday I shall soon begin." Apparently he never did, though; and no translations of either poet by him have ever been found in his papers.

Still, Williams drew strength from his reading and study of Lorca. He learned to trust his own instincts. As he concludes in his essay about the influences that made Lorca: "The old forms were bred and made for song. The man spent his life singing. That is the forgotten greatness of poetry, that it was made to be sung—but it has been divorced from the spoken language by the pedants." Moving forward with his own work, Williams took this wisdom with him. His long and productive collaboration with New Directions had started in 1937, along with his friendship with James

Laughlin, who that year published his second novel *White Mule*. The following year, he published his *Complete Collected Poems*, further establishing his reputation as a poet.

Also in the late 1930s, Williams was working with his bedridden octogenarian mother, who lived with him, on their translation from the Spanish of *The Dog and the Fever;* translating this bawdy satire attributed to Quevedo was an attempt to "amuse" and "divert" her with conversation (recorded in a notebook and later used to write *Yes, Mrs. Williams*). He told Zukofsky about the novella, originally published in 1625: "Innuendo, scandal, double meaning, obscenity, filth, contempt for woman, peasant humor, proverbs, anti-clericalism are blended into a hodgepodge of soup, goats, chamber pots until Gertrude Stein seems a simple, quiet mind beside them."[*]

The Spanish Civil War did much to inspire Williams's translations of both poetry and prose from Spain during this period, including his essay on Lorca that went through many drafts until he achieved its finished form. It was in an early draft that he articulated the following vision, which he chose to set aside and not include in the published work: "If more of the Spanish were better translated—more in the spirit of modern American letters, using word of mouth and no literary english—most of the principles which have been so hard won, the directness, the immediacy, the reality of our present day writing in verse and prose would be vitally strengthened. Our efforts away from vaguely derived, nostalgic effects so deleterious to the mind would be replaced by the directness and objectivity we so painfully seek."

---

[*]Later, in the mid-1940s, Williams described *The Dog and the Fever* to Laughlin as "far more 'modern' than ever Hemingway or even Gertie [Stein] ever thought of being" and as "absolutely 'new directions' in its manner of writing and hot as hell besides." He said it was "the first recorded use of the pure image to tell a story."

```
If more of the Spanish were better translated - more in the
spirit of modern American letters, #### using word of mouth and
no literary english - most of the principles which have been so
hard won, the directness, the immediacy, the reality of our
present day writing in verse and prose would be vitally strength-
ened. Our efforts away from vaguely derived,  nostalgic effects
so deleterious to the mind, would be replaced by the directness
and objectivity we so painfully seek.
```

Here, too, Williams defines his approach to verse translation; the very same modernist approach seen in the earlier poems he translated with his father for *Others*.

Sweated Blood / 1940s & '50s

This section contains Williams's translations of exclusively Latin American poets, including aboriginal singers. These translations parallel the technical maturity and experimentation of his own poetry post-1939, the year he recognized as the turning point in his poetic life. The section opens with his translation of Luis Palés Matos's "Prelude in Boricua," made in the wake of his visit to Puerto Rico in April 1941. There, he met the poem's author who, like him, aimed to write poetry using the vernacular around him. He had traveled to the island to be a guest speaker at the First Inter-American Writers' Conference of the University of Puerto Rico. It was his first time in his mother's homeland. Surely, the experience touched him deeply, especially the Hispanic faces of the people, the local architecture, and the spoken Spanish in the air.

He concluded his talk at the conference, titled "An Informal Discussion of Poetic Form," by saying: "If, in a work of art, it is by the nascent form that the fullest and most timely significance is expressed, what function might not Latin America exercise toward the United States and Canada in this respect? To introduce us to Spanish and Portuguese literature—pure and simple. And if to that literature, to make us familiar with its forms as contrasted with our own. For instance: *What* influence can Spanish have on us who speak a derivative of English in North America? To shake us free for a reconsideration of the poetic line."

While in Puerto Rico, Williams also met poet-translator Muna Lee, one of the principal organizers of the writers' conference. Her poems had appeared in *Others*, during the days of his involvement with the magazine. It was Lee who, in 1942, introduced him to the poetry of Jorge Carrera Andrade, to which he responded: "The images are as you say so extraordinarily clear, so related to the primitive that I think I am seeing as an aborigine saw and sharing that lost view of the world." Sixteen years later, Williams would translate Carrera Andrade himself. His rendering of "Dictated by the Water" gave him the chance to pursue his own preoccupation with objects and with conceptualizing sensuous experience. Not only did he find in Carrera Andrade's work a genuine American voice, he found what had become most important to him as a poet—his lifelong quest— namely, the chance "to get a form without deforming the language" (*I Wanted to Write a Poem*). He found the work of a poet who had mastered the use of images presented by means of direct colloquial speech.

In the spring of 1958, after Williams had just completed the fifth and final book of his epic *Paterson*, he was visited at his home by Rutgers professor José Vázquez-Amaral, who went there to pick up translations of contemporary Latin American poets that Williams made for him. Vázquez-Amaral had recently won a Rockefeller Foundation grant to promote new writing from Latin America in the United States and, as he explained in a letter to Williams, one of his objectives was "to encourage translations . . . by eminently qualified people like yourself." He emphasized: "Only in this way do I feel that the cause of better knowledge of Latin American literature is served." His first magazine project was done as co-guest-editor of the Latin American feature of *New World Writing,* published later that year. He had asked Williams to translate the work of several poets, including Carrera Andrade, Pablo Neruda, Nicanor Parra, Alí Chumacero, Álvaro Figueredo, Silvina Ocampo, Ernesto Mejía Sánchez, and Eugenio Florit. Space limitations in this issue ultimately prevented the publication of all of Williams's translations. One of the translations not included was Mejía Sánchez's "Vigils," which during his visit Vázquez-Amaral read aloud. Williams responded positively, and said it sounded good, noting he had "sweated blood" to make it.

Vázquez-Amaral was the motivating force behind Williams's translations of Latin American poets made in the latter half of the 1950s. Early in that decade, in 1951, Vázquez-Amaral, destined to become famous in literary circles as the translator of Pound's *Cantos* into Spanish, initiated a correspondence with Williams. In his first letter to the poet, in which he introduced himself and stated his desire to meet with him to discuss ways to advance inter-American literary exchange, Vázquez-Amaral said: "I have received the following 'anonymous communication' [i.e., from Pound, with whom he was in contact]: 'Dr. W. Carlos Williams is near you, at 9 Ridge Rd, Rutherford, N. J. An honest man, who has spent most of his life in Rutherford, he is part spanish, and has for 50 years been meaning to translate MORE spanish into north-american. J.V.A. would do well to call on him, and Old Bill might help to stir up some enthusiasm at Rutgers." Vázquez-Amaral at the time was struggling at Rutgers to gain greater respect for Spanish, long the orphan of French and Italian in the Romance Languages Department (in 1971, he became founding chairman of the new Spanish and Portuguese Department).

Although the decade of the Second World War had seen another flourishing of translations of Latin American poets, including New Directions' landmark *Anthology of Contemporary Latin-American Poetry*, for which Williams recommended the inclusion of work by Luis Palés Matos, Nicolás Guillén, Emilio Ballagas, and others, the dominant formalist New Criticism and the Cold War conspired to limit widespread appreciation of these poets. It was, finally, in 1956 that Vázquez-Amaral told Williams: "The time is now ripe, I believe, for the pioneering work you mentioned to me in your letter of December 17, 1951. The work of cultural interpenetration between English and Spanish America seems to have arrived." Two years later, he received the Rockefeller grant that enabled him to pursue his dream and to work with Williams on translation projects.

Vázquez-Amaral selected the poems, then sent Williams the Spanish texts, along with literal translations he himself had made "to save [Williams] some useless trouble." Williams's job was to "make them into poems." He met the task with determination, as he told Galway Kinnell in a letter just weeks before the visit by Vázquez-Amaral described above: "I have been handed a job which I let myself in for without suspecting how hard it would be, the translation of about twelve longish poems from Spanish into English. It has me nailed to the mast. . . . [S]ome difficult passages I can spend the whole day on before I can find a solution."

By "nailed to the mast" Williams meant that, like those

captains of sailing ships who fought battles at sea with their colors nailed to the mast to tell their opponent they wouldn't yield or surrender, he was engaged in a creative struggle with poetry he wouldn't abandon. Beyond that, the phrase unfurls his very identity as poet, his defining colors. He had used the same phrase nearly a half century earlier to define his other identity, as physician, in a letter to his brother Edgar about establishing his medical practice at their parents' house in Rutherford: "My office will be furnished and my shingle 'nailed to the mast'—nothing short of that— like Perry's flag at the battle on Lake Erie." And nothing short of that, as well, when it came to poetry, the translation of which was always an appealing challenge for him. Finding solutions to difficult passages offered him the thrill of victory.

Also during the spring of 1958, Vázquez-Amaral was asking Williams to do translations of Mexican poetry for Donald Allen's *Evergreen Review*. He was preparing an issue that would feature work by writers and artists in a selective cross section, to be called "The Eye of Mexico." This issue, planned for autumn, finally came out in the winter of the following year. It included Williams's translations of two poems by Chumacero. Allen had hoped to include his translation of Octavio Paz's "Hymn Among the Ruins," and asked him to make it, sending him a published literal prose rendering on which to base the verse translation. Paz himself was delighted by the prospect of Williams translating his poem. But the publication of Williams's translation did not take place in that magazine. It happened a decade-plus later, when New Directions included it in Paz's book of early poems.

"From My Window" is verse by his mother, Elena. He included it in his "personal record" of her, *Yes, Mrs.*

Williams, published in 1959. This poem is clearly not a work of literary genius, but of another, more personal nature. No one asked him to translate it or, for that matter, to write this book about her. He did it for himself and his posterity, to preserve her memory, as in his renderings of her many Spanish proverbs on which he was raised, and which he included in the book, such as:

> *Malo, Malo, Malo, Malo! Si te conocia en el falo.*
> Bad, bad, bad, bad, if they know you in your
>   weakness.
> *El que se hace de miel, se lo comen las hormigas.*
> He who makes himself honey will be eaten by
>   the ants.
> *Mas vale caer en gracio que ser gracioso.*
> Better to stumble into grace than to be a clown.
> *No hay mal que dure cien años. Ni cuerpo que*
>   *lo resiste.*
> There is no evil that lasts a hundred years.
>   Nor body which can bear it.

Like her humble poem of lost dreams, these proverbs collectively embody his mother's character and spirit. All originate in the language of his beginnings. They further reveal the bicultural aspect of himself, in particular his essential Hispanic part named Carlos that found expression in his Spanish translations.

The final poem here, "To W.C.W.," based on Eunice Odio's homage, came about in the fall of 1959. Again, Vázquez-Amaral was intimately involved in the process. Not only did he provide a literal translation, he had brought the beautiful Odio to Williams's home to meet him. The poem resulted from her visit. It followed the crippling stroke Williams had the previous October, and the subsequent months of his despair and physical struggle, during which time he had difficulty speaking, concentrating, walking, and writing. He taught himself to speak again and learned to type with his unparalyzed hand on an electric typewriter. Surely, the act of giving voice to this poem enabled him to affirm himself poetically. In this self-portrait, his creative departures from the literal text reveal his own particular sense of who he was—or wanted to be—as both a man and poet.

*
* *

This compilation of Williams's translations of Spanish and Latin American poetry expands his established canon in a significant way. It adds previously unknown work and also work that hasn't yet been properly recognized as his. More than that, in bringing these verse translations together, it shows in full force his many Hispanic personae, which collectively span his entire poetic life. These translations indeed are dramatic masks he wore in the performance of poetry, to render Spanish voices in his beloved American idiom, with the stamp of his own personality. Paul Mariani emphasized to me in correspondence that Williams's interest in making translations from the Spanish continued throughout his life—"from his early collaborations with his father, right through to his last poems, in which he speaks of Neruda's influence." Yet the fruits of his long-time interest are not widely known, nor appreciated. They can be now. Mariani further encouraged this book when he told me it "will reinforce the sense of Williams as one deeply invested in the language and rhythm of the New World—North as well as South." It also underscores his deep connection with the literature of Spain. At the center of these translations is his distinctive genius; the individual poems he translated are, in many ways, reflections of his own poetic quest. Collected in a single volume, Williams's poems from the Spanish contribute to a fuller understanding of his literary achievement as a translator and poet. The sheer beauty of his great lyric performances is, in itself, something to enjoy in honor of him.

JONATHAN COHEN
New York, 2011

By Word of Mouth

POEMS FROM THE SPANISH
1916-1959

All this fits well into my scheme. I don't care
how I say what I must say. If I do original work
all well and good. But if I can say it (the matter
of form I mean) by translating the work of
others that also is valuable. What difference
does it make?

—WCW

Others /1916

FRAGMENTO DE "LAS IMPOSIBLES"

A los estudiantes de Honduras y de Nicaragua.

Soy el primer amor. Soy el encanto,
soy el dolor de aquella forma blanca
de cuando os embozaba vuestro manto
y estudiabais aquí y en Salamanca.

La mujer es dolor. Pero de todas
yo soy la que más hiere y ciega y trunca.
Yo soy la primer noche de las bodas
del alma, a que ninguno llegó nunca.

Yo lancé mis miradas como halcones
a todas esas almas virginales
que fácil presa dan a las mujeres.
Yo soy la que sonríe en los balcones,
llenos de luna, de los arrabales
a los poetas y a los bachilleres.

A veces fui la prima, primo hermano,
blanca como la flor del limonero
y cuando me rozabais a la mano
me concedía más que un cuerpo entero.

Mi boca acaso di. Mas ten seguro
de que si la besasteis, fue sólo una
vez, a caballo sobre el muro
y estaba tan envuelta por la luna,

que cuando os vi marchar ibais beodo,
alta la frente, en la sonrisa el ruego

FRAGMENTS OF "LAS IMPOSIBLES"

To the students of Honduras and Nicaragua.

I am the first love. I am the enchantment.
I am the pain of that white form
the time when you wrapped yourself in your cloak
and studied here or in Salamanca.

Woman is pain. But of all
I am she who worst wounds and blinds and maims.
I am the first night of the nuptials
of the soul, to which none ever came.

I launch my glances like falcons
to all those virgin souls
that give easy prey to women.
I am she who smiles on the balconies
full of the moon, in the outskirts
to the poets and the freshmen.

Sometimes I was the cousin, cousin mine,
white as the flower of the lemon tree
and when you brushed my hand
you gave me more than a body entire.

Perhaps I gave you my mouth. But be sure
that if you kissed it, it was only once
astride the wall
and I so closely wrapped against the moon

that when I saw you go you went drunk,
forehead high, in your smile a prayer

y besabais el aire; e ibais ciego
de mí, como una luz que estaba en todo.

Estudiantes, vosotros los que Honduras
o Nicaragua envía a Guatemala
y que juntáis ensueños y apreturas
y vivís tres o cuatro en una sala;

purpúrea inmigración de juventudes;
mitad bohemios y mitad troveros,
sonoros de preludios de laúdes,
luminosos de sangre de luceros,

que todos conocéis la copa loca
y dos meses debéis a los patrones;
yo soy aquella rubia colegiala
que con un beso que os dejó en la boca,
prendió en vuestros omóplatos una ala
y puso el Sol en vuestros corazones.

—*Rafael Arévalo Martínez*

and you kissed the air; and you went
blinded by me as by a light shining in all things.

Students, you whom Honduras
or Nicaragua sends to Guatemala
and who mingle dreams and penury
and live three or four in a room;

crimson immigration of youths
half bohemians and half singers
sonorous with the preludes of lutes,
luminous with the blood of stars,

who all know the mad cup
and stand two months in your landlord's debt:
I am that golden-haired school girl
who, with a kiss which she left on your mouth,
pinned a wing to your shoulders
and put the sun in your hearts.

MI VIDA ES UN RECUERDO

Cuando la conocí me amé a mí mismo.
Fue la que tuvo mi mejor lirismo,
la que encendió mi obscura adolescencia,
la que mis ojos levantó hacia el cielo.

Me humedeció su amor, que era una esencia,
doblé mi corazón como un pañuelo
y después le eché llave a mi existencia.

Y por eso perfuma el alma mía
con lejana y diluida poesía.

—*Rafael Arévalo Martínez*

MY LIFE IS A MEMORY

When I met her I loved myself.
It was she who had my best singing,
she who set flame to my obscure youth,
she who raised my eyes toward heaven.

Her love moistened me, it was an essence.
I folded my heart like a handkerchief
and after I turned the key on my existence.

And thus it perfumes my soul
with a distant and subtle poetry.

SENSACIÓN DE UN OLOR

Oh de los rostros sabios que he llevado a mis labios
    como vinos traidores.
Las mujeres sencillas que senté en mis rodillas como
    ramos de flores.

Y sobre todo una, de cabellera bruna, que parecía flor
y que dejó en mi vida la vaga, la diluida sensación de un
    olor.

Sus ojos de diamante, tenían la inquietante mirada del no
    ser
y me dio la más fuerte sensación de la muerte que me dio
    una mujer
y la más encendida sensación de la vida que he podido
    tener.

—*Rafael Arévalo Martínez*

THE SENSATION OF A SMELL

Oh the wise faces I have carried to my lips like treacher-
 ous wines.
The simple women I have seated on my knees like
 branches of flowers.

And above all one, with brown hair, who resembled a
 flower
and who left in my life the vague sensation of a smell.

Her diamond eyes had the disquieting look of non-
 existence
and she gave me the strongest sensation of death I have
 had of a woman
and the most burning sense of life that I have been able
 to obtain.

LA CANCIÓN DEL CAMINO

Era un camino negro.
La noche estaba loca de relámpagos. Yo iba
en mi potro salvaje
por la montaña andina.
Los chasquidos alegres de los cascos,
como masticaciones de monstruosas mandíbulas,
destrozaban los vidrios invisibles
de las charcas dormidas.
Tres millones de insectos
formaban una como rabiosa inarmonía.

Súbito, allá, a lo lejos,
por entre aquella mole doliente y pensativa
de la selva,
vi un puñado de luces como tropel de avispas.
¡La posada! El nervioso
látigo persignó la carne viva
de mi caballo, que rasgó los aires
con un largo relincho de alegría.

Y como si la selva
lo comprendiese todo, se quedó muda y fría.

Y hasta mí llegó, entonces,
una voz clara y fina
de mujer que cantaba. Cantaba. Era su canto
una lenta . . . muy lenta . . . melodía:
algo como un suspiro que se alarga
y se alarga y se alarga . . . y no termina.

Entre el hondo silencio de la noche
y a través del reposo de la montaña, oíanse

THE SONG OF THE ROAD

It was a black road.
The night was mad with lightnings. I was riding
my wild colt
over the Andean range.
The cheery strokes of the hoofs
like the chewing of monstrous jaws
shattered the invisible glass
of the sleeping pools.
Three million insects
made seemingly a mad discord.

Suddenly, there, in the distance
within that sad and pensive mass
of the wood,
I saw a handful of lights like a swarm of wasps.
The inn! The nervous
lash struck the living flesh
of my horse, who split the air
with a long neigh of joy.

And as if the wood
understood all, it remained mute and cold.

And there reached me then
the voice of a woman
clear and fine, singing. She sang. Her song was
a slow . . . very slow . . . melody:
something like a sigh which lengthens
and lengthens and lengthens . . . and does not end.

In the deep silence of the night
above the repose of the mountain, I heard

los acordes
de aquel canto sencillo de una música íntima,
como si fuesen voces que llegaran
desde la otra vida . . .

Sofrené mi caballo;
y me puse a escuchar lo que decía.

—Todos llegan de noche,
todos se van de día . . .

Y formándole dúo,
otra voz femenina
completó así la endecha
con ternura infinita:

—El amor es tan sólo una posada
en mitad del camino de la Vida . . .

Y las dos voces luego
a la vez repitieron con amargura rítmica:
—Todos llegan de noche,
todos se van de día . . .

Entonces, yo bajé de mi caballo
y me acosté en la orilla
de una charca.
Y fijo en ese canto que venía
a través del misterio de la selva,
fui cerrando los ojos al sueño y la fatiga.
Y me dormí arrullado; y, desde entonces,
cuando cruzo las selvas por rutas no sabidas,
jamás busco reposo en las posadas;

the notes
of that simple song of intimate music,
as if it were voices coming
from the other life . . .

I reined in my horse
and listened to what they were saying.

—All come with the night,
all go with the day.

And forming a duet
another woman's voice
thus completed the verse
with consummate tenderness:

—Love is only an inn
midway in the road of life . . .

And afterward the two voices
repeated together with rhythmic bitterness:
—All come with the night
all go with the day . . .

Then, I descended from my horse
and laid myself down at the edge
of a pool.
And intent upon this song which came
through the mystery of the forest
I closed my eyes before sleep and fatigue.
And fell asleep to the singing: and from that time,
when I cross the forests by unknown ways,
I never seek repose in the inns

y duermo al aire libre mi sueño y mi fatiga,
porque recuerdo siempre
aquel canto sencillo de una música íntima:

—Todos llegan de noche,
todos se van de día.
El amor es tan sólo una posada
en mitad del camino de la Vida . . .

—*José Santos Chocano*

but I sleep off in the free air my sleepiness and my fatigue,
because I always remember
that simple song of intimate music:

—All come with the night
all go with the day . . .
Love is only an inn
midway in the road of life!

SEÑOR, YO PIDO UN HUERTO

Señor, yo pido un huerto en un rincón tranquilo
donde haya una quebrada con aguas abundantes,
una casita humilde cubierta de campánulas,
y una mujer y un hijo que sean como Vos.

Yo quisiera vivir muchos años, sin odios,
y hacer como los ríos que humedecen la tierra
mis versos y mis actos frescos y de puros.
Señor, dadme un sendero con árboles y pájaros.

Yo deseo que nunca os llevéis a mi madre,
porque a mi me gustara cuidarla cual a un niño
y dormirla con besos, cuando ya viejecita
necesite del sol.

Quiero tener buen sueño, algunos pocos libros,
un perro cariñoso que me salte a las piernas,
un rebaño de cabras, toda cosa silvestre,
y vivir de la tierra labrada por mis manos.

Salir a la campiña y florecer en ella;
sentarme por la tarde, bajo el rústico alero,
a beber aire fresco y oloroso a montaña,
y hablarle a mi pequeño de las cosas humildes.

Por la noche contarle algún cuento sencillo,
enseñarle a reír con la risa del agua
y dormirle pensando en que pueda, a la tarde,
guardar esa frescura de la hierba embebida;

LORD, I ASK A GARDEN

Lord, I ask a garden in a quiet spot
where there may be a brook with a good flow,
an humble little house covered with bell-flowers
and a wife and a son who shall resemble Thee.

I should wish to live many years, free from hates,
and make my verses, as the rivers
that moisten the earth, fresh and pure.
Lord, give me a path with trees and birds.

I wish that you would never take my mother,
for I should wish to tend her as a child
and put her to sleep with kisses, when somewhat old
she may need the sun.

I wish to sleep well, to have a few books,
an affectionate dog that will spring upon my knees,
a flock of goats, all things rustic,
and to live of the soil tilled by my own hand.

To go into the field and flourish with it;
to seat myself at evening under the rustic eaves,
to drink in the fresh mountain perfumed air
and speak to my little one of humble things.

At night to relate to him some simple tale,
teach him to laugh with the laughter of water
and put him to sleep thinking that he may later on
keep that freshness of the moist grass.

y luego, al otro día, levantarme a la aurora
admirando la vida, bañarme en la quebrada,
ordeñar a mis cabras en la dicha del huerto,
y agregar una estrofa al poema del mundo.

—*Alfonso Guillén Zelaya*

And afterward, the next day, rise with dawn
admiring life, bathe in the brook,
milk my goats in the happiness of the garden
and add a strophe to the poem of the world.

VERSOS A LA LUNA

¡Oh, luna, que hoy te asomas al tejado
de la iglesia, en la calma tropical,
para que te salude un trasnochado
y te ladren los perros de arrabal!

¡Oh, luna! . . . En tu silencio te has burlado
de todo! . . . En tu silencio sideral,
viste anoche robar en despoblado
. . . y el ladrón era un Juez Municipal! . . .

Mas tú ofreces, viajera saturnina,
con qué elocuencia en los espacios mudos
consuelo al que la vida laceró,

mientras te cantan, en cualquier cantina,
neurasténicos bardos melenudos
y piojosos, que juegan dominó . . .

—*Luis Carlos López*

VERSES TO THE MOON

Oh moon, who now look over the roof
of the church, in the tropical calm
to be saluted by him who has been out all night,
to be barked at by the dogs of the suburbs,

Oh moon, who in your silence have laughed at
all things! In your sidereal silence
when, keeping carefully in the shadow, the
municipal judge steals from some den.

But you offer, saturnine traveler,
with what eloquence in mute space
consolation to him whose life is broken,

while there sing to you from a drunken brawl
long-haired, neurasthenic bards,
and lousy creatures who play dominos.

EL MAL DEL SIGLO

El paciente:

Doctor, un desaliento de la vida
que en lo íntimo de mí se arraiga y nace,
el mal del siglo . . . el mismo mal de Werther,
de Rolla, de Manfredo y de Leopardi.
Un cansancio de todo, un absoluto
desprecio por lo humano . . . un incesante
renegar de lo vil de la existencia
digno de mi maestro Schopenhauer;
un malestar profundo que se aumenta
con todas las torturas del análisis . . .

El médico:

—Eso es cuestión de régimen: camine
de mañanita; duerma largo; báñese;
beba bien; coma bien; cuídese mucho;
¡lo que usted tiene es hambre!

—*José Asunción Silva*

THE DISEASE OF THE CENTURY

The Patient:

Doctor, a discouragement of life
which is in my intimate self rooted and born,
the disease of the century . . . that same disease of Werther,
of Rolla, of Manfred and of Leopardi.
A weariness with all things, an absolute
contempt for the human, an incessant
revolt at the vileness of existence
worthy of my master Schopenhauer;
a profound unrest which grows
with all the tortures of analysis.

The Doctor:

—This is a matter of regimen; walk
in the early morning; sleep long, take baths;
drink well; eat well; take good care of yourself;
the thing that ails you is hunger!

And Spain Sings / 1930s

CANCIÓN

Alivia sus fatigas
El labrador cansado
Quando su yerta barba escarcha cubre,
Pensando en las espigas
Del Agosto abrasado,
Y en los lagares ricos del Octubre.

—*Lupercio de Argensola*

CANCION

The tired workman
Takes his ease
When his stiff beard's all frosted over
Thinking of blazing
August's corn
And the brimming wine-cribs of October.

LÁGRIMAS QUE NO PUDIERON

Lágrimas que no pudieron
Tanta dureza ablandar,
Yo las volveré a la mar,
Pues que de la mar salieron.

Heme en lágrimas deshecho,
Que la mar de amor me ha dado,
Y habré de salir a nado,
Pues mar del amor se han hecho:
Lágrimas que así crecieron
Sin poder a vos llegar,
Yo las volveré a la mar,
Pues que de la mar salieron.

Hicieron en duras peñas
Mis lágrimas sentimiento,
Tanto que de mi tormento
Dieron unas y otras señas;
Pero pues ellas no fueron
Bastantes a os ablandar,
Yo las volveré a la mar,
Pues que de la mar salieron.

—*Anonymous*

TEARS THAT STILL LACKED POWER

Tears that still lacked power
To lessen such cruelty
I will return them to the sea
Since from the sea they have come.

Of tears I've an overplus
With which love's sea has endowed me,
Till I must swim to be free
Since love, a sea, has o'erflowed me;
Tears that still mounting higher
To reach you still lacked the sum
I will return them to the sea
Since from the sea they have come.

In the face of harsh opposition
Tears bitterly wrung
Have sought this or that token
As much as torment could find tongue;
But since not all were availing
To lessen such cruelty,
I will return them to the sea
Since from the sea they have come.

ALAMOS DEL PRADO

Alamos del prado,
Fuentes de Madrid,
Como estoy ausente
Murmurais de mí.

Todos van diciendo
Mis tristes congojas,
El viento en las hojas
Las fuentes corriendo:
A todos diciendo
Lisongera os ví,
Como estoy ausente
Murmurais de mí.

Con razon me espanto
Dando al despediros
Las plantas suspiros,
Y las aguas llanto;
Que fingierais tanto
Nunca lo creí,
Como estoy ausente
Murmurais de mí.

Estando en presencia
Música me hicistes,
Luego me vendistes
Que vistes mi ausencia:
Dios me dé paciencia,
Mientras peno aquí,
Como estoy ausente
Murmurais de mí.

—*Anonymous*

30

POPLARS OF THE MEADOW

Poplars of the meadow
Fountains of Madrid
That I am absent now
You murmur complaints of me.

All of you are saying
How sorry my chance is
The wind in the branches
The fountains playing
To all men conveying
I knew you once happy.
That I am absent now
You murmur complaints of me.

Justly may I wonder
Since at my leaving
The plants with sighs were heaving
And all tears the waters;
That you were such liars
I never thought could be.
That I am absent now
You murmur complaints of me.

Being in your presence
Music you'd waken
Later I'm forsaken
When you discover my absence.
May God give me patience
Here in my misery,
That I am absent now
You murmur complaints of me.

VERDADES

Verdades diré en camisa
Poco menos que desnudas.

—*Francisco de Quevedo*

TRUTHS

I give you truths in chemises
(said he)
Not far from naked.

MUCHOS DICEN MAL DE MÍ

Muchos dicen mal de mí,
Y yo digo mal de muchos:
Mi decir es más valiente,
Por ser tantos, y ser uno.

—Francisco de Quevedo

MANY SPEAK ILL OF ME

Many speak ill of me
And I of many a one.
My speech is the braver
They are many, I'm alone.

VIENTO DEL PUEBLO

Sentado sobre los muertos
que se han callado en dos meses,
beso zapatos vacíos
y empuño rabiosamente
la mano del corazón
y el alma que lo mantiene.
Que mi voz suba a los montes
y baje a la tierra y truene,
eso pide mi garganta
desde ahora y desde siempre.
Acércate a mi clamor,
pueblo de mi misma leche,
árbol que con tus raíces
encarcelado me tienes,
que aquí estoy yo para amarte
y estoy para defenderte
con la sangre y con la boca
como dos fusiles fieles.
Si yo salí de la tierra,
si yo he nacido de un vientre
desdichado y con pobreza,
no fue sino para hacerme
ruiseñor de las desdichas,
eco de la mala suerte,
y cantar y repetir
a quien escucharme debe
cuanto a penas, cuanto a pobres,
cuanto a tierra se refiere.
Ayer amaneció el pueblo
desnudo y sin qué ponerse,
hambriento y sin qué comer,

WIND OF THE VILLAGE

Seated above the dead
who are silent these two months
I kiss empty shoes
and grasp furiously
the heart's hand
and of the soul that supports it.
Let my voice lift to the mountains
and crash to the earth again in thunder
is my throat's supplication
from this day and forever.
Draw near to my clamor
village of the same milk as I,
tree that with its roots
holds me imprisoned,
for I am here myself to show my love
and here to defend you
with my blood as with word of mouth
that are as two faithful rifles.
If I was born of this earth,
if I have issued from a womb
wretched and impoverished,
it was only that I might be
the nightingale of misfortunes,
echo of evil luck,
to sing over and over
for those who must hear,
all that to poverty, all that to anguish,
all that to country is referred.
Yesterday the people wakened
naked and with nothing to wear,
hungry with nothing to eat,

y el día de hoy amanece
justamente aborrascado
y sangriento justamente.
En su mano los fusiles
leones quieren volverse
para acabar con las fieras
que lo han sido tantas veces.
Aunque te falten las armas,
pueblo de cien mil poderes,
no desfallezcan tus huesos,
castiga a quien te malhiere
mientras que te queden puños,
uñas, saliva, y te queden
corazón, entrañas, tripas,
cosas de varón y dientes.
Bravo como el viento bravo,
leve como el aire leve,
asesina al que asesina,
aborrece al que aborrece
la paz de tu corazón
y el vientre de tus mujeres.
No te hieran por la espalda,
vive cara a cara y muere
con el pecho ante las balas,
ancho como las paredes.
Canto con la voz de luto,
pueblo de mí, por tus héroes:
tus ansias como las mías,
tus desventuras que tienen
del mismo metal el llanto,
las penas del mismo temple
y de la misma madera
tu pensamiento y mi frente,

and today has dawned
heavily tormented
bleeding in fact.
With guns in their hands
they wish themselves lions
to put an end to the savage beasts
who would ruin them as before.
Although you lack arms
village of ten times ten thousand powers
concede no rest to your bones,
punish those who dastardly wound you,
while you are possessed of fists,
nails, spit, and there lives in you
heart, guts,
a man's parts, and your teeth.
Brave as the wind is brave,
and light as the lightest airs,
kill those who would kill you,
hate him who hates
the peace of your hearts,
and the wombs of your women.
Don't let them wound you from behind
live face to face with them and die
with chests to the bullets
as broad as a wall.
I sing with the voice of a lute,
for your heroes, my own village,
your anguish one with my own,
your misfortunes that are made
of the same metal and weeping,
suffering of the same stock,
the same fiber
your thoughts and my own,

tu corazón y mi sangre,
tu dolor y mis laureles.
Antemuro de la nada
esta vida me parece.
Aquí estoy para vivir
mientras el alma me suene,
y aquí estoy para morir,
cuando la hora me llegue,
en los veneros del pueblo
desde ahora y desde siempre.
Varios tragos es la vida
y un solo trago es la muerte.

—*Miguel Hernández*

your heart and my blood,
your grief and the laurels which I bring.
An outer buttress to nothingness
seems this life to me.
I am here to live but
while the soul lies sleeping,
and here to die
when my hour shall come,
in the bosom of my people,
from now on and forever.
Life is drunk over and over
and death is one swallow only.

JUANELO DE LAVIANA

¡Aquí mis hombres, aquí,
a la conquista de Oviedo!
Que si Oviedo se resiste,
más se resiste en su cerco.
Que sepan en toda España
que si no es todavía nuestro
es porque la dinamita
de los valientes mineros
no quiere ver la ciudad
convertida en cementerio.
Pastores de Pravia vienen,
pescadores y labriegos
en armas contra el traidor
que de sed se está muriendo.
Aranda, el traidor Aranda,
ya no puede con el peso
de su traición, que hay quien dice
que se le ha vuelto veneno.
¡Aquí mis hombres, aquí,
a la conquista de Oviedo!
A las avanzadas nuestras,
junto a la línea de fuego,
con piano de manubrio
llegó el valiente Juanelo.
"Oíd 'La Internacional,'
oídla, mis compañeros,
que les queda poca vida
a los verdugos del pueblo;
que si Oviedo se resiste,
más se resiste en su cerco."
Un puñado de metralla
dejó al pianillo deshecho;
pero "La Internacional"

JOHNNY OF LAVIANA

Here, men, here,
to the taking of Oviedo!
For if Oviedo holds out
we shall hold out the longer.
It is known throughout Spain
that if it is not yet taken
it is because the dynamite
of the valiant miners
does not wish to make
a cemetery of the city.
Shepherds of Pravia come,
fishermen and laborers,
in arms against the traitor
who is dying of thirst.
Aranda, the traitor Aranda,
can no longer hold out,
because of the weight of
his treason, which has turned
to venom, they say, within him.
Here, men, here,
to the taking of Oviedo.
Hard on our advance,
close to the line of fire,
comes the valiant Johnny
bringing a hand organ.
"Hear 'The International,'
hear it, my companions,
that there be short life
to the hangmen of the town;
for if Oviedo holds out
we shall hold out the longer."
A burst of shrapnel
made splinters of the hand organ;

sonaba en todos los pechos,
que no han de callarla, no,
mientras quede en pie un minero.
La artillería enemiga
no cesó en su cañoneo:
hondas simas las granadas
en la tierra iban abriendo.
Con un viejo acordeón
volvió el valiente Juanelo,
corriendo entre los pistones
la alegría de sus dedos.
"Oíd 'La Internacional,'
oídla, mis compañeros,
y haced que vuestros disparos
sean cada vez más certeros;
que si Oviedo se resiste,
más se resiste en su cerco."
Polvo y tierra removida
hicieron callar al viejo
acordeón que cantaba
junto a los sacos terreros.
Entre las avanzadillas
pasó el valiente Juanelo;
puso la bandera roja
en un laurel, a despecho
de los disparos que hacían
los traidores, y en silencio
cogió de nuevo el fusil
para combatir de nuevo.
"¡Aquí mis hombres, aquí,
a la conquista de Oviedo;
que si Oviedo se resiste,
más se resiste en su cerco!"

—*Rafael Beltrán Logroño*

but "The International"
was still deeply heard,
for it will not be silenced, no,
while a miner is left standing.
The enemy guns
continue their cannonade:
deep caverns are opened
in the earth by the shells.
With an old accordion
the valiant Johnny returns,
the laughter of his fingers
running among the keys.
"Hear 'The International,'
hear it, my companions,
and see to it that your aim
proves each time more deadly;
for if Oviedo holds out,
we shall hold out the longer."
Dust and flying earth
silenced the old
accordion which sang
close to the sandbags.
Out beyond the advance
went the valiant Johnny;
fixed the red flag
to a laurel, despite
the shots of
the traitors, and in silence
picked up a rifle
to join the fight once more.
"Here, men, here,
to the taking of Oviedo;
for if Oviedo holds out,
we shall hold out the longer!"

JUAN MONTOYA

El bordón ha enmudecido,
que hablaron las escopetas,
y el palo y el martinete
se han hecho gritos de guerra.
Las hoces piden gargantas,
gargantas de sangre negra.
Trigo de hogaño—¡buen trigo!—
por espigas, las cabezas.
Ni tratos ni chalaneos,
ni se rían las tijeras:
cada bostezo que peguen
ensoñando con peleas,
un señorito en el suelo
dando "bocaos" en la tierra.
Quede quieta la guitarra,
encima la cantarera
llorando cintas moradas,
por mordaza la cejuela.
Pon el calzón en la cruz
pregonando tu entereza,
que éste es negocio de hombres
con la hombría muy bien puesta.
La mejilla del retaco
en tu mejilla morena,
y la venganza en los ojos;
la bala . . . ¡donde la sueñas!
¡En el mismo corazón
del corazón de la fiera!
Hila barbechos dormidos,
olivares lagartea,
bebe caminos en curva,

JUAN MONTOYA

The refrain is grown silent,
now that the guns have spoken,
and the songs of the people
are turned to shouts of war.
The scythes plead for throats,
throats of blackest blood.
Wheat of today! good wheat!
the spikes of it, heads now.
No selling nor shrewd bargains,
nor laughter of the shears,
each yawn that they give
is a dream now of battle,
some pretty gentleman fallen,
stretched biting the dust.
The guitar remains unheard,
over the jar-shelf on the wall,
its purple ribbons weeping,
choked where it's hung.
Sling your breeches on the cross
proclaiming yourself won,
that this is business for a man,
with heavy stress upon manhood.
The lank cheek of the gunstock
upon your own dark cheek,
and vengeance in your eyes;
the bullet! where you dream it!
into that very heart
the heart of a savage beast!
File through the fallow land,
lizardlike in the olive groves,
drink the curving highways,

que te amparen las caderas
de los montes. Dale al viento
rabias para que se encienda.
Que el dolor de veinte siglos
te levante la cabeza
hecho garra gavilana,
que te aciguate la presa.
¡La presa tuya, ganada
en veinte siglos de espera!
¡Ay, Juan Montoya, gitano,
gitano de pura cepa!
¡¡Quién te ha visto miliciano
con un civil a la vera . . . !!

—*Mariano del Alcázar*

that the flanks of the mountains
may protect you. Give the wind
fury for it to burst into flame.
That twenty centuries of anguish
raise up your head
become the talons of a hawk
to strike your prey dead.
Your very prey, possessed
after twenty centuries of waiting.
Ah, Juan Montoya, gypsy,
gypsy of purest stock!
Who could have believed you'd take arms,
you, so thorough a civilian.

UNA NIÑA BONITA

Una niña bonita.
Se asomó a su balcón.
Ella me pidió el alma,
Yo la di el corazón,
Ella me pidió el alma,
Y yo la dije adiós.

—*Anonymous*

A PRETTY GIRL

A pretty girl
Showed herself at the balcony
Asked me for my soul
I gave her my heart
Asked me for my soul
I said good-bye.

Sweated Blood /
1940s & '50s

_____

PRELUDIO EN BORICUA

Tuntún de pasa y grifería
y otros parejeros tuntunes.
Bochinche de ñañiguería
donde sus cálidos betunes
funde la congada bravía.

Con cacareo de maraca
y sordo gruñido de gongo,
el telón isleño destaca
una aristocracia macaca
a base de funche y mondongo.

Al solemne papaluá haitiano
opone la rumba habanera
sus esguinces de hombro y cadera,
mientras el negrito cubano
doma la mulata cerrera.

De su bachata por las pistas
vuela Cuba, suelto el velamen,
recogiendo en el caderamen
su áureo niágara de turistas.

(Mañana serán accionistas
de cualquier ingenio cañero
y cargarán con el dinero . . .)

Y hacia un rincón—solar, bahía,
malecón o siembra de cañas—
bebe el negro su pena fría

PRELUDE IN BORICUA*

Mixup of kinkhead and high yaller
And other big time mixups.
Messaround of voodoo chatter
Where their warm black bodies
Loosen the savage conga.

With crowing of the maraca
And heavy grunt of the gongo
The island curtain goes up on
An aristocracy macaca
Based in trip and corn pone.

To the solemn haitian God-be-praised
Is opposed the rumba habanera
With its angular hips and shoulders
While the cuban negrito
Takes on his hot-foot mulatta.

From her jamboree, taking the trail,
Flies Cuba, all sails set
To gather on her haunches
The golden tourist Niagara.

(Tomorrow they'll be shareholders
In some sugar mill
And take over with the money . . .)

And in whatever corner—lot, bay,
Pier or cane-field—
The negro drinks his cold portion

*Boricua, here, means "Puerto Rican" (speech); for more about the name,
see Annotations, p. 148.

alelado en la melodía
que le sale de las entrañas.

Jamaica, la gorda mandinga,
reduce su lingo a gandinga.
Santo Domingo se endominga
y en cívico gesto imponente
su numen heroico respinga
con cien odas al Presidente.
Con su batea de ajonjolí
y sus blancos ojos de magia
hacia el mercado viene Haití.
Las antillas barloventeras
pasan tremendas desazones,
espantándose los ciclones
con matamoscas de palmeras.

¿Y Puerto Rico? Mi isla ardiente,
para ti todo ha terminado.
En el yermo de un continente,
Puerto Rico, lúgubremente,
bala como cabro estofado.

Tuntún de pasa y grifería,
este libro que va a tus manos
con ingredientes antillanos
compuse un día . . .

. . . y en resumen, tiempo perdido,
que me acaba en aburrimiento.
Algo entrevisto o presentido,
poco realmente vivido
y mucho de embuste y de cuento.

—*Luis Palés Matos*

Consoled by the melody
That springs from his own bowels.

Jamaica, the heavy tub-of-guts
Switches her lingo to guts enough.
Santo Domingo dolls herself up
And with imposing civic gesture
Stirs her heroic genius
To a hundred presidential odes.
With her tray of penny candy
And white magic eyes
Comes Haiti to the market.
The Windward Islands are made up
Of overwhelming disgusts
To astonish the cyclones
With their fly-swatter palm trees.

And Puerto Rico? My burning island
For thee all has indeed ended.
Among the shambles of a continent
Puerto Rico, lugubriously
You bleat like a roast goat.

Mixup of black boy and high yaller,
This book to your hands
With ingredients from the Antilles
Sum up a day . . .

. . . and in short, lost time,
that leaves me heavy headed.
Something drawn out or reported,
Little really lived
And much of pretension and hearsay.

TRES POEMAS NÁHUATL

Tus cantos reúno:
    como esmeraldas los ensarto:
hago con ellos un collar:
el oro de las cuentas está duro:
adórnate con ellas.
    ¡Es en la tierra tu riqueza única!
Se emparejan las plumas de quetzal,
y erguidas están hacia arriba
las de verdinegro y rojo color:
con ellas tú pintas tu atabal.
    ¡Es en la tierra tu riqueza única!

¿Adónde habré de ir, adónde habré de ir?
    —¡Está el camino escarpado, el camino escarpado
del Dios—Dos! ¿No acaso todos nosotros
allá do están los despojados de la carne
en el interior del cielo?
    Desde esta tierra al lugar de los descarnados,
juntos nos vamos, juntos nos vamos a su casa:
nadie queda en la tierra,
¿quién hay que decir pueda:
donde estáis, oh vosotros, mis amigos?

¿Vendrá otra vez, acaso, el príncipe, el Aguila
    Cacamatl?
¿Vendrá otra vez, acaso, Ayocuan, el que flechó
    el cielo?
¿Aun ellos os darán placer?
    ¡No dos veces nos vamos:
    una sola vez para siempre nos vamos!
Me pongo a llorar lleno de tristeza:

THREE NAHUATL POEMS

One by one I proclaim your songs:
    I bind them on, gold crabs, as if they were anklets:
    like emeralds I gather them.
Clothe yourself in them: they are your riches.
    Bathe in feathers of the quetzal,
your treasury of birds' plumes, black and yellow,
the red feathers of the macaw
beat your drums about the world:
deck yourself out in them: they are your riches.

Where am I to go, whither?
    The road's there, the road to Two-Gods.
    Well, who checks men here,
here where all lack a body,
at the bottom of the sky?
Or, maybe, it is only on Earth
that we lose the body?
    Cleaned out, rid of it completely,
His House: there remains none on this earth!
Who is it that said:
Where find them? our friends no longer exist!

Will he return will Prince Cuautli ever return?
Will Ayocuan, the one who drove an arrow
    into the sky?
Shall these two yet gladden you?
    Events don't recur: we vanish once only.
Hence the cause of my weeping:

El príncipe Ayocuan era el jefe de guerra,
nos regía con dureza, no tenía otro afán que su orgullo,
no tenía otro anhelo que ser tenido en precio sobre otros.
    ¡Ya no es su tiempo ahora: ya no viene a conocer
al que es ahora nuestro padre y nuestra madre!
Me pongo a llorar: ¡se fué, se fué allá do están los
    descarnados!

—*Anonymous*

Prince Ayocuan, warrior chief
governed us harshly.
His pride waxed more, he grew haughty
here among men.
    But his time is finished . . .
he can no longer come to bow down before Father and
    Mother. . . .
This is the reason for my weeping:
He has fled to the place where all lack a body.

HIMNO ENTRE RUINAS

Donde espumoso el mar siciliano . . .
> —Góngora

Coronado de sí el día extiende sus plumas.
¡Alto grito amarillo,
caliente surtidor en el centro de un cielo
imparcial y benéfico!
Las apariencias son hermosas en esta su verdad
    momentánea.
El mar trepa la costa,
se afianza entre las peñas, araña deslumbrante;
la herida cárdena del monte resplandece;
un puñado de cabras es un rebaño de piedras;
el sol pone su huevo de oro y se derrama sobre el mar.
Todo es dios.
¡Estatua rota,
columnas comidas por la luz,
ruinas vivas en un mundo de muertos en vida!

Cae la noche sobre Teotihuacán.
En lo alto de la pirámide los muchachos fuman
    marihuana,
suenan guitarras roncas.
¿Qué yerba, qué agua de vida ha de darnos la vida,
dónde desenterrar la palabra,
la proporción que rige al himno y al discurso,
al baile, a la ciudad y a la balanza?
El canto mexicano estalla en un carajo,
estrella de colores que se apaga,
piedra que nos cierra las puertas del contacto.
Sabe la tierra a tierra envejecida.

HYMN AMONG THE RUINS

Where foams the Sicilian sea . . .
                    —Góngora

Self crowned the day displays its plumage.
A shout tall and yellow,
impartial and beneficent,
a hot geyser into the middle sky!
Appearances are beautiful in this their momentary
        truth.
The sea mounts the coast,
clings between the rocks, a dazzling spider;
the livid wound on the mountain glistens;
a handful of goats becomes a flock of stones;
the sun lays its gold egg upon the sea.
All is god.
A broken statue,
columns gnawed by the light,
ruins alive in a world of death in life!

Night falls on Teotihuacán.
On top of the pyramid the boys are smoking
        marijuana,
harsh guitars sound.
What weed, what living waters will give life to us,
where shall we unearth the word,
the relations that govern hymn and speech,
the dance, the city and the measuring scales?
The song of Mexico explodes in a curse,
a colored star that is extinguished
a stone that blocks our doors of contact.
Earth tastes of rotten earth.

Los ojos ven, las manos tocan.
Bastan aquí unas cuantas cosas:
tuna, espinoso planeta coral,
higos encapuchados,
uvas con gusto a resurrección,
almejas, virginidades ariscas,
sal, queso, vino, pan solar.
Desde lo alto de su morenía una isleña me mira,
esbelta catedral vestida de luz.
Torres de sal, contra los pinos verdes de la orilla
surgen las velas blancas de las barcas.
La luz crea templos en el mar.

Nueva York, Londres, Moscú.
La sombra cubre al llano con su yedra fantasma,
con su vacilante vegetación de escalofrío,
su vello ralo, su tropel de ratas.
A trechos tirita un sol anémico.
Acodado en montes que ayer fueron ciudades,
*   Polifemo bosteza.*
Abajo, entre los hoyos, se arrastra un rebaño de hombres.
(Bípedos domésticos, su carne
—a pesar de recientes interdicciones religiosas—
es muy gustada por las clases ricas.
Hasta hace poco el vulgo los consideraba animales impuros.)

Ver, tocar formas hermosas, diarias.
Zumba la luz, dardos y alas.
Huele a sangre la mancha de vino en el mantel.
Como el coral sus ramas en el agua
extiendo mis sentidos en la hora viva:
el instante se cumple en una concordancia amarilla,
¡oh mediodía, espiga henchida de minutos,
copa de eternidad!

Eyes see, hands touch.
Here a few things suffice:
prickly pear, coral and thorny planet,
the hooded figs,
grapes that taste of the resurrection,
clams, stubborn maidenheads,
salt, cheese, wine, the sun's bread.
An island girl looks on me from the height of her duskiness,
a slim cathedral clothed in light.
A tower of salt, against the green pines of the shore,
the white sails of the boats arise.
Light builds temples on the sea.

New York, London, Moscow.
Shadow covers the plain with its phantom ivy,
with its swaying and feverish vegetation,
its mousy fur, its rats swarm.
Now and then an anemic sun shivers.
Propping himself on mounts that yesterday were cities,
        Polyphemus yawns.
Below, among the pits, a herd of men dragging along.
(Domestic bipeds, their flesh—
despite recent religious prohibitions—
is much-loved by the wealthy classes.
Until lately people considered them unclean animals.)

To see, to touch each day's lovely forms.
The light throbs, all darties and wings.
The wine-stain on the tablecloth smells of blood.
As the coral thrusts branches into the water
I stretch my senses to this living hour:
the moment fulfills itself in a yellow harmony.
Midday, ear of wheat heavy with minutes,
eternity's brimming cup.

Mis pensamientos se bifurcan, serpean, se enredan,
recomienzan,
y al fin se inmovilizan, ríos que no desembocan,
delta de sangre bajo un sol sin crepúsculo.
¿Y todo ha de parar en este chapoteo de aguas muertas?

¡Día, redondo día,
luminosa naranja de veinticuatro gajos,
todos atravesados por una misma y amarilla dulzura!
La inteligencia al fin encarna,
se reconcilian las dos mitades enemigas
y la conciencia-espejo se licúa,
vuelve a ser fuente, manantial de fábulas:
Hombre, árbol de imágenes,
palabras que son flores que son frutos que son actos.

—Octavio Paz

My thoughts are split, meander, grow entangled,
start again,
and finally lose headway, endless rivers,
delta of blood beneath an unwinking sun.
And must everything end in this spatter of stagnant water?

Day, round day,
shining orange with four-and-twenty bars,
all one single yellow sweetness!
Mind embodies in forms,
the two hostile become one,
the conscience-mirror liquifies,
once more a fountain of legends:
man, tree of images,
words which are flowers become fruits which are deeds.

ODA A LA PEREZA

Ayer sentí que la oda
no subía del suelo.
Era hora, debía
por lo menos
mostrar una hoja verde.
Rasqué la tierra: "Sube,
hermana oda
—le dije—
te tengo prometida,
no me tengas miedo,
no voy a triturarte,
oda de cuatro hojas,
oda de cuatro manos,
tomarás té conmigo.
Sube,
te voy a coronar entre las odas,
saldremos juntos, por la orilla
del mar, en bicicleta."
Fue inútil.

Entonces,
en lo alto de los pinos,
la pereza
apareció desnuda,
me llevó deslumbrado
y soñoliento,
me descubrió en la arena
pequeños trozos rotos
de sustancias oceánicas,
maderas, algas, piedras,
plumas de aves marinas.

ODE TO LAZINESS

Yesterday I felt this ode
would not get off the floor.
It was time, I ought
at least
show a green leaf.
I scratch the earth: "Arise,
sister ode
—said to her—
I have promised you,
do not be afraid of me,
I am not going to crush you,
four-leaf ode,
four-hand ode,
you shall have tea with me.
Arise,
I am going to crown you among the odes,
we shall go out together along the shores
of the sea, on a bicycle."
It was no use.

Then,
on the pine peaks,
laziness
appeared in the nude,
she led me dazzled
and sleepy,
she showed me upon the sand
small broken bits
of ocean substance,
wood, algae, pebbles,
feathers of sea birds.

Busqué sin encontrar
ágatas amarillas.
El mar
llenaba los espacios
desmoronando torres,
invadiendo
las costas de mi patria,
avanzando
sucesivas catástrofes de espuma.
Sola en la arena
abría un rayo
una corola.
Vi cruzar los petreles plateados
y como cruces negras
los cormoranes
clavados en las rocas.
Liberté una abeja
que agonizaba en un velo de araña,
metí una piedrecita
en un bolsillo,
era suave, suavísima
como un pecho de un pájaro,
mientras tanto en la costa,
toda la tarde,
lucharon sol y niebla.
A veces
la niebla se impregnaba
de luz
como un topacio,
otras veces caía
un rayo de sol húmedo
dejando caer gotas amarillas.

I looked for but did not find
yellow agates.
The sea
filled all spaces
crumbling towers,
invading
the shores of my country,
advancing
successive catastrophes of the foam.
Alone on the sand
spread wide
its corolla.
I saw the silvery petrels crossing
and like black creases
the cormorants
nailed to the rocks.
I released a bee
that was agonizing in a spider's net.
I put a little pebble
in my pocket,
it was smooth, very smooth
as the breast of a bird,
meanwhile on the shore,
all afternoon
sun struggled with mist.
At times
the mist was steeped
in thought,
topaz-like,
at others fell
a ray from the moist sun
distilling yellow drops.

En la noche,
pensando en los deberes de mi oda
fugitiva,
me saqué los zapatos
junto al fuego,
resbaló arena de ellos
y pronto fui quedándome
dormido.

—*Pablo Neruda*

At night,
thinking of the duties of my fugitive ode,
I pull off my shoes
near the fire;
sand slid out of them
and soon I began to fall
asleep.

ODA A LOS CALCETINES

Me trajo Maru Mori
un par
de calcetines
que tejió con sus manos
de pastora,
dos calcetines suaves
como liebres.
En ellos
metí los pies
como en
dos
estuches
tejidos
con hebras del
crepúsculo
y pellejo de ovejas.

Violentos calcetines,
mis pies fueron
dos pescados
de lana,
dos largos tiburones
de azul ultramarino
atravesados
por una tranza de oro
dos gigantescos mirlos,
dos cañones:
mis pies
fueron honrados
de este modo
por

ODE TO MY SOCKS

Maru Mori brought me
a pair
of socks
that she knitted with her own hands
of a shepherdess,
two soft socks
you'd say they were rabbits.
In them
I stuck my feet
as in
two
jewel cases
woven
with threads of
twilight
and lamb skins.

Violent socks,
my feet were
two fish
made of wool,
two long sharks
of ultramarine blue
shot
with a tress of gold
two gigantic blackbirds,
two cannons:
my feet
were honored
in this manner
by

estos
celestiales
calcetines.
Eran
tan hermosos
que por primera vez
mis pies me parecieron
inaceptables
como dos decrépitos
bomberos, bomberos
indignos
de aquel fuego
bordado,
de aquellos luminosos
calcetines.

Sin embargo
resistí
la tentación aguda
de guardarlos
como los colegiales
preservan
las luciérnagas,
como los eruditos
coleccionan
documentos sagrados,
resistí
el impulso furioso
de ponerlos
en una jaula
de oro
y darles cada día
alpiste

these
celestial
socks.
They were
so beautiful
that for the first time
my feet seemed to me
unacceptable
like two decrepit
firemen, firemen
unworthy
of that embroidered
fire,
those luminous
socks.

Nevertheless
I resisted
the acute temptation
to keep them
as schoolboys
keep
fireflies,
or the erudite
collect
sacred documents,
I resisted
the furious impulse
to put them
in a cage
of gold
and to feed them
every day

y pulpa de melón rosado.
Como descubridores
que en la selva
entregan el rarísimo
venado verde
al asador
y se lo comen
con remordimiento,
estiré
los pies
y me enfundé
los
bellos
calcetines
y
luego los zapatos.

Y es ésta
la moral de mi oda:
dos veces es belleza
la belleza
y lo que es bueno es doblemente
bueno
cuando se trata de dos calcetines
de lana
en el invierno.

—*Pablo Neruda*

bird seed
and the pulp of rosey
melon.
Like discoverers
who in the forest
yield the very rare
green deer
to the spit
and with regret
eat it,
I stretched out
my feet
and pulled over them
the
beautiful
socks
and
then my shoes.

And this is
the moral of my ode:
twice beautiful
is beauty
and what is good is twice
good
when it is two socks
made of wool
in winter.

LOS OJOS VERDES

Solemnidad de tigre incierto, ahí en sus ojos
vaga la tentación y un náufrago
se duerme sobre jades pretéritos que aguardan
el día inesperado del asombro
en épocas holladas por las caballerías.

Ira del rostro, la violencia
es río que despeña en la quietud el valle,
azoro donde el tiempo se abandona
a una corriente análoga a lo inmóvil, bañada
en el reposo al repetir
la misma frase desde la sílaba primera.

Sólo el sonar bajo del agua insiste
con incesante brío, y el huracán acampa
en la demora, desterrado
que a la distancia deja un mundo de fatiga.

Si acaso comprendiéramos, epílogo
sería el pensamiento o música profana,
acorde que interrumpe ocios
como la uva aloja en vértigo el color
y la penumbra alienta a la mirada.

Vayamos con unción a la taberna donde
aroma el humo que precede,
bajemos al prostíbulo a olvidar esperando:
porque al fin contemplamos la belleza.

—*Alí Chumacero*

GREEN EYES

Solemnity of a bemused tiger, there in his eyes
temptation goes wandering and a shipwrecked man
sleeps on a hoary pillow of jade
the unwaited day of marvels
in ages which herds of horses have trampled.

A furious face, violence
is a river tumbled upon quietness in the valley,
awe where time abandons itself
to a motionless current, bathed
in rest repeating
the same phrase over and over from the first syllable.

Only a sound beneath the water insists
with loud clamor, and tardy precincts
of the hurricane, its exile
leaving a world fatigued and remote.

If perchance we understand, the epilogue
would be the thought of a world music,
languors broken by a chord
as the grape in a vertiginous shower
casts shadows confusing the eye.

With decorum let us proceed to the inn
where the smoke of our cigars has preceded us,
let us go to the brothel while waiting:
for at last beauty awaits us.

MONÓLOGO DEL VIUDO

Abro la puerta, vuelvo a la misericordia
de mi casa donde el rumor defiende
la penumbra y el hijo que no fue
sabe a naufragio, a ola o fervoroso lienzo
que en ácidos estíos
el rostro desvanece. Arcaico reposar
de dioses muertos llena las estancias,
y bajo el aire aspira la conciencia
la ráfaga que ayer mi frente aún buscaba
en el descenso turbio.

No podría nombrar sábanas, cirios, humo
ni la humildad y compasión y calma
a orillas de la tarde, no podría
decir "sus manos," "mi tristeza," "nuestra tierra"
porque todo en su nombre
de heridas se ilumina. Como señal de espuma
o epitafio, cortinas, lecho, alfombras
y destrucción hacia el desdén transcurren,
mientras vence la cal que a su desnudo niega
la sombra del espacio.

Ahora empieza el tiempo, el agrio sonreír
del huésped que en insomnio, al desvelar
su ira, canta en la ciudad impura
el calcinado són y al labio purifican
fuegos de incertidumbre
que fluyen sin respuesta. Astro o delfín, allá
bajo la onda el pie desaparece,
y túnicas tornadas en emblemas
hunden su ardiente procesión y con ceniza
la frente me señalan.

—*Alí Chumacero*

WIDOWER'S MONOLOGUE

I open the door, return to the familiar mercy
of my own house where a vague
sense protects me the son who never was
smacking of shipwreck, waves or a passionate cloak
whose acid summers
cloud the fading face. Archaic refuge
of dead gods fills the region,
and below, the wind breathes, a conscious
gust which fanned my forehead yesterday
still sought in the perturbed present.

I could not speak of sheets, candles, smoke
nor humility and compassion, calm
at the afternoon's edges, I could not
say "her hands," "her sadness," "our country"
because everything in her name
is lighted by her wounds. Like a signal sprung
of foam, an epitaph, curtains, a bed, rugs
and destruction moving toward disdain
while the lime triumphs denying her nakedness
the color of emptiness.

Now time begins, the bitter smile
of the guest who in sleeplessness sings,
waking his anger, within the vile city
the calcined music with curled lip
from indecision
that flows without cease. Star or dolphin, yonder
beneath the wave his foot vanishes,
tunics turned to emblems
sink their burning shows and with ashes
score my own forehead.

EL VIAJE DE LA TRIBU

Otoño sitia el valle, iniquidad
desborda, y la sacrílega colina al resplandor
responde en forma de venganza. El polvo mide
y la desdicha siente quien galopa
adonde todos con furor golpean:
prisionero asistir al quebrantado círculo
del hijo que sorprende al padre contemplando
tras la ventana obstruida por la arena.

Sangre del hombre víctima del hombre
asedia puertas, clama: "Aquí no existe nadie,"
mas la mansión habita el bárbaro que busca
la dignidad, el yugo de la patria
interrumpida, atroz a la memoria,
como el marido mira de frente a la mujer
y en el cercano umbral la huella ajena apura
el temblor que precede al infortunio.

Hierro y codicia, la impotente lepra
de odios que alentaron rapiñas e ilusiones
la simiente humedece. Al desafío ocurren
hermano contra hermano y sin piedad
tornan en pausa el reino del estigma:
impulsa la soberbia el salto hacia el vacío
que al declinar del viento el águila abandona
figurando una estatua que cayó.

Volcada en el escarnio del tropel
la tarde se defiende, redobla la espesura
ante las piedras que han perdido los cimientos.
Su ofensa es compasión cuando pasamos

THE WANDERINGS OF THE TRIBE

Autumn surrounds the valley, iniquity
overflows, and the hill sacred to splendor
responds in the form of a revenge. The dust measures
and misfortune knows who gallops
where all gallop with the same fury:
constrained attendance on the broken circle
by the son who startles his father gazing
from a window buried in the sand.

Blood of man's victim
besieges doors, cries out: "Here no one lives,"
but the mansion is inhabited by the barbarian who seeks
dignity, yoke of the fatherland
broken, abhorred by memory,
as the husband looks at his wife face to face
and close to the threshold, the intruder
hastens the trembling that precedes misfortune.

Iron and greed, a decisive leprosy
of hatreds that were fed by rapine and deceits
wets the seeds. Brother against brother
comes to the challenge without pity
brings to a pause its stigma against the kingdom of pity:
arrogance goads the leap into the void
that as the wind dies the eagles abandon
their quest like tumbled statues.

Emptied upon the mockery of the crowd
the afternoon defends itself, redoubles its hide
against stones that have lost their foundations.
Her offense is compassion when we pass

de la alcoba dorada a la sombría
con la seguridad de la pavesa: apenas
un instante, relámpago sereno cual soldado
ebrio que espera la degradación.

De niños sonreímos a la furia
confiando en el rencor y a veces en la envidia
ante el rufián que de improviso se despide
y sin hablar desciende de la bestia
en busca del descanso. El juego es suyo,
máscara que se aparta de la escena, catástrofe
que ama su delirio y con delicia pierde
el último vestigio de su ira.

Vino la duda y la pasión del vino,
cuerpos como puñales, aquello que transforma
la juventud en tiranía: los placeres
y la tripulación de los pecados.
Un estallar alzaba en la deshonra
el opaco tumulto y eran las cercanías
ignorados tambores y gritos y sollozos
a los que entonces nadie llamó "hermanos."

Al fin creí que el día serenaba
su propia maldición. Las nubes, el desprecio,
el sitio hecho centella por la amorosa frase,
vajilla, aceite, aromas, todo era
un diestro apaciguar al enemigo,
y descubrí después sobre el naufragio tribus
que iban, eslabones de espuma dando tumbos
ciegos sobre un costado del navío.

—*Alí Chumacero*

from the gilded alcove to the somber one
with the fixety of glowing coals: hardly
a moment, peaceful light as upon
a drunken soldier awaiting his degradation.

We can smile later at our childish furies
giving way to rancor and sometimes envy
before the ruffian who without a word taking leave
descends from the beast
in search of surcease. The play is his:
mask quitting the scene, catastrophy
overtaking love with its delirium and with delight
looses the last remnant of its fury.

Came doubt and the lust for wine,
bodies like daggers, that transform
youth to tyranny: pleasures
and the crew of sin.
A bursting rain of dishonor
a heavy tumult and the nearnesses
were disregarded drums and cries and sobs
to those whom no one calls by the name of "brother."

At last I thought the day calmed
its own profanities. The clouds, contempt,
the site made thunderbolts by love's phrases,
tableware, oil, sweet odors, was all
a cunning propitiation of the enemy,
and I discovered later floating over
the drowned tribes, links of foam tumbling
blindly against the sides of a ship.

SOLO DE PIANO

Ya que la vida del hombre no es sino una acción a distancia,
Un poco de espuma que brilla en el interior de un vaso;
Ya que los árboles no son sino muebles que se agitan:
No son sino sillas y mesas en movimiento perpetuo;
Ya que nosotros mismos no somos más que seres
(Como el dios mismo no es otra cosa que dios)
Ya que no hablamos para ser escuchados
Sino para que los demás hablen
Y el eco es anterior a las voces que lo producen;
Ya que ni siquiera tenemos el consuelo de un caos
En el jardín que bosteza y que se llena de aire,
Un rompecabezas que es preciso resolver antes de morir
Para poder resucitar después tranquilamente
Cuando se ha usado en exceso de la mujer;
Ya que también existe un cielo en el infierno,
Dejad que yo también haga algunas cosas:

Yo quiero hacer un ruido con los pies
Y quiero que mi alma encuentre su cuerpo.

—*Nicanor Parra*

PIANO SOLO

Since man's life is nothing but a bit of action at a distance,
A bit of foam shining inside a glass;
Since trees are nothing but moving trees:
Nothing but chairs and tables in perpetual motion;
Since we ourselves are nothing but beings
(As the godhead itself is nothing but God);
Now that we do not speak solely to be heard
But so that others may speak
And the echo precede the voice that produces it;
Since we do not even have the consolation of a chaos
In the garden that yawns and fills with air,
A puzzle that we must solve before our death
So that we may nonchalantly resuscitate later on
When we have led woman to excess;
Since there is also a heaven in hell,
Permit me to propose a few things:

I wish to make a noise with my feet
I want my soul to find its proper body.

DESNUDO

La azul la benemérita
de su cauce de alondras o de espuma
naciendo sin cesar
latiendo marmolísima
allí donde el ombligo
mediterráneo impone
su majestad y lanza
a la mejilla al pie círculos de oro
avanza Sirio entre ambos senos que
imparten dudas órdenes al viento
dormida está la azul apacentando
la lentitud del eco entre sus muslos
ahora que abro la siesta para verla
horizontal estricta gobernando
los enjambres las fraguas los viñedos
la embelesada flauta los glaciares
azulazul los gallos
de las veletas cuando
su noble vientre aísla
el curso del océano
dormida está la joven cazadora
y un abedul germina en su rodilla.

—*Álvaro Figueredo*

NAKED

The azure yielder
of the skylark's way or the foam
ceaselessly re-created
made into ultimate marble
there where the mediterranean
navel imposes
its majesty and casts
precious strokes of gold upon cheeks
advanced by Sirius between
two breasts that give
hard commands to the wind
asleep in the blue shepherding
slowness between her thighs
now that I part them a siesta to see her
strictly disciplined horizontals
crowds forges vineyard country
instant shadows glaciers
blueblue cocks
of weather vanes when
their noble bellies isolate
the flow of the ocean as
the young huntress sleeps
and a birch tree quickens upon her knees.

LOS CABALLOS INFINITOS

Los he visto dormidos sobre el pasto,
repetirse acostados en los campos;
furiosos los he visto, arrodillados,
como dioses altivos, todos blancos,
vestidos y con cintas, y salvajes
con crines como el pelo desatado
de sirenas antiguas en las playas.
Las víboras con ellos han soñado,
los juncos y las madres acostadas
los temían debajo de las palmas.
Trémulos anunciaban las batallas,
anunciaban el miedo y la constancia,
como el redoble del tambor trotaban,
como un aplauso en un profundo teatro.
Vieron sangrar heridas en el barro,
murieron entre flores, en los charcos,
visitados por aves y gusanos.
Se acercaban trayendo hombres amados,
se acercaban con hórridos tiranos,
revestidos de púrpura y de sangre.
Recordaré caballos implacables:
los tarpanes de Rusia; los Przewalski;
los ciento veinte nombres de caballos
que hay en Roma, grabados en un mármol;
en el Olimpo de Dionisio de Argos,
con un duro pentámetro en el flanco,
de bronce afrodisíaco, el caballo
cuyo amor cautivaba a los caballos
que acudían al Altis; el que amaba
tanto Semíramis, la reina de Asia;
los que probaron con fruición arcana—

THE INFINITE HORSES

I have seen them asleep on the grass,
mirroring themselves in the fields;
seen them furious, on their knees,
like haughty gods, all white,
dressed in ribbons, savage
with manes flying like the loose hair
of legended sirens on the shores.
Vile vipers have dreamt of them,
reeds and bedded mothers
keep them closed in the palms.
Trembling they foretell battles,
like the beat of their trotting hoofs,
like applause thundering in a vast theater.
They have seen wounds bleeding into the clay,
died among flowers, in the mire,
intimates of birds and vermin.
They draw near bearing armed men,
approach on their backs vile tyrants,
dressed in blood and purple.
I shall remember implacable horses:
Russian trappings; the Przewalski;
the names of the hundred and twenty
Roman horses, chiseled in marble;
at the Olympus of Dionus of Argus,
with a hard penumbra aphrodisiac on
their bronze flanks, the horse
most favored by the others
was that of Altis; he who was so loved
by Semiramis, the queen of Asia;
those who tasted with blessed transports—

mucho antes que los chinos las probaran—
del té las verdes hojas inspiradas;
construido por Virgilio ese caballo
cuya sombra virtuosa tan amable
conseguía sanar a los caballos.
Recordaré en un cielo anaranjado
caballos en la sombra iluminados,
uniendo ansiosamente a los amantes
en grutas apacibles de distancia.

—*Silvina Ocampo*

long before the Chinese tasted them—
green tea from those inspired leaves;
that horse created by Virgil
whose benign and virtuous shadow was gifted
with the power to heal all horses.
I shall remember in an orange sky,
horses so left in shadow,
concernedly bringing lovers together
in peaceful grottoes from a distance.

LOS DESVELOS

I

Días en blanco ¿qué sería
de mí? Mientras cae la noche
en el pecho soñado, cuántos
pasos inciertos hacen blanco,
enemiga. Caer como la noche
sin engaño, en cualquier lecho
que el azar nos propone, en busca
de la caricia más recatada y blanca.
Dime tú, alma mía, elogiada
o favorecida, amiga del señor
en la noche estrellada, cómo
borrar el día cegado por su luz.

II

Días en blanco ¿qué sería
de mí? Libre como el corcel
ante la meta infinita, jadeante
sin caer, libre del muro
que nos pusieron ciego, pero
con el orgullo de quien pone
todo lo que de sí puede
poner el hombre—libre,
si puede ser, no maldecido—
sabiendo que ahora estoy
aquí y mañana . . . ni dónde
ni cuándo ni mañana. Libre,
libre como el puñal pero con-
tigo, sufriéndote, negándote,
callándote el poder de la más
fiera conciencia y sin embargo

VIGILS

I

Vacant days, what shall become
of me? At nightfall
already conquered in our dreams,
facing a wall, uncertain we stumble
and go astray. To fall as night falls
without deceit, on any bed
which chance interposes, in search
of the most modest and white caress.
Tell me, my soul, elect
or favored, friend of the Lord
in the star filled night, how
bar the day from that blinding light.

II

Vacant days, what shall become
of me? Free as the steed
before the timeless goal, panting
but secure, free of the wall
placed about us blind, but
with the pride of one who gives
all that of himself that may be
given by a free man,
uncursed if it may be—,
knowing that I am here
today, and tomorrow . . . no where,
nor when, failing tomorrow. Free,
as a dagger, but with
you, suffering, self pitied,
keeping from self the power of
a most savage conscience and, for

amado, temido sin descanso.
Cuando te deposito, mi cuerpo,
en la noche del bien, ahí obs-
curecido renazco y me calumnio.

III
Días en blanco ¿qué sería
de mí? Al borde de la luz
más repentina y ácida, arena
envanecida por el rayo, como
la espuma al filo de las
olas iba mi corazón entre
vaivenes, de tumbo en tumbo
hacia la estrella. Qué blancura
más sigilosa, qué maravilla
insomne, las rocas de cal
viva, las aguas que la furia
hace palidecer, la plata gritando
en el crisol que no se apaga.
Días sólo con nieve dibujados.
Días como la luna endurecidos
por la mirada de la cobra
y el llanto derritiendo la nieve
egoísta del pecho más amado.
Oh implacable, oh feroz blanco
entre el gris y el aire, entre el agua
y el gris, pero brillante, dañino,
humillante, con el brillo del homicida,
así los huesos que dejaré labrados
y pulidos de señal en la noche.

all that, relentless love.
When I place you, my body,
sacrificial to night's beneficence,
lowly I am reborn and humble me.

III
Vacant days, what shall become
of me? Bordered by a light
acid and sudden, sand
made vain by a lightning, like
foam at the edges of waves
to my heart's thumps
swinging from bump to bump
toward the star. What whiteness
so stealthy, what sleepless
wonder, the live lime
rocks, the furious waters
cause to blanch, silver shouting
from the torch which never dims.
Bays solely blossomed in snow.
Days hardened by the moon
as if at a cobra's gaze
and weeping melting the self
centered snow of meanest breast.
Oh implacable! Oh ferocious white
between grey and the air, shading water
to grey, shining, threatening,
debasing, with a murderous glint,
thus are the bones I shall leave
polished as a signal in the night.

IV

Estoy arrodillado ante el muro
blanco. Escribo mi nombre
sobre el agua. Veo pasar
las horas como nubes. No hay
fondo. No hay abismo.
A mis pies disminuye la sombra.
¿Quién soy? ¿No me conoces?
¿Qué extraño monstruo me
está sorbiendo el poco de
tiniebla que necesito para no
desaparecer? ¿Qué delirio
los dioses huraños me regalan?
Estoy en mí fuera de sí,
contigo, niebla mía, mi
ceniza, mi descendencia, mi
cuerpo, mírame la última vez
antes que me destruya.

V

Alguien me llama y no sé responder.
No estoy. No he regresado. No soy yo.
Subterfugios, desconocida persona,
cuerpo extraño que seguirá llamando
desde siempre hasta nunca sin jamás.
No estoy. No me conozco. ¿Quién es quién?
Llamo, imploro, interrogo, no contesta,
y seguiré llamando ¿a quién? y quién
a quién, sin fin y sin principio,
hasta que pueda llamar y responder
a la vez, con una sola vez.

IV

I am kneeling before the white wall
I write my name
upon the water. I see the hours
passing like clouds. There is no
bottom. Neither abyss.
At my feet shadow draws back.
Who am I? Do you not know me?
What strange monster
is sucking the minuscule
darkness that I need not
disappear? What delirium
the Uranian skies have willed on me?
I am within myself beside myself,
side by side, my fog, my
ashes, my breed, my
guts, look upon me for the last time
before I destroy myself.

V

Someone calls me and I don't know how to answer.
I am not here. I have not returned. It is not I.
Subterfuge, unknown person,
unknown self who will continue calling
from always to never without stop.
I am not here. I am unknown to myself. Who is who?
I call, implore, question, no answer,
and I will continue calling, whom? and who
to whom, without end or beginning,
until I can call and answer
with one voice and at the same time.

VI

Qué veloz pensamiento
me lanzó al corazón,
el corazón a Ti. Qué
dicha no negada.
Qué asombro. Dentro
de su corteza la vida
guardaba las formas
exteriores, como el huevo,
anterior a sí mismo.
Quise a la vez lo que
quise y no quise—
recordar, ser desleal
al presente—y consentir
¿qué más da? que sólo Tú
me quemes las entrañas.

VII

El dolor no significa
movimiento ni el placer
inmovilidad. Tan quieta-
mente oscilo entre el
daño y el gozo que
ya no sé si vivo
o desfallezco. Hazme
que gire o permanezca.

—*Ernesto Mejía Sánchez*

VI

What plunging thoughts
the heart casts upon me,
your own heart. What
patent joy.
What amazement. Under
its bark life has
kept its forms by which
we know it, the egg
from which it was borne.
I desire what at once
I desire and spurn
—to remember, be false to
the present—and consent,
what difference? by you alone
my entrails are scorched.

VII

Pain does not point
either to movement or
movelessness. Thus
sway dancing between
the hurt and the joy
so that I no longer know
whether I live
or swoon. Let me spin
if I would persist.

DICTADO POR EL AGUA

I

Aire de soledad, dios transparente
que en secreto edificas tu morada
¿en pilares de vidrio de qué flores?
¿sobre la galería iluminada
de qué río, qué fuente?
Tu santuario es la gruta de colores.
Lengua de resplandores
hablas, dios escondido,
al ojo y al oído.
Sólo en la planta, el agua, el polvo asomas
con tu vestido de alas de palomas
despertando el frescor y el movimiento.
En tu cabello azul van los aromas.
Soledad convertida en elemento.

II

Fortuna de cristal, cielo en monedas,
agua, con tu memoria de la altura,
por los bosques y prados
viajas con tus alforjas de frescura
que guardan por igual las arboledas
y las hierbas, las nubes y ganados.
Con tus pasos mojados
y tu piel de inocencia
señalas tu presencia
hecha toda de lágrimas iguales,
agua de soledades celestiales.
Tus peces son tus ángeles menores
que custodian tesoros eternales
en tus frías bodegas interiores.

DICTATED BY THE WATER

I

Solitude, transparent god
who in secret keep your abode
among pillars of glass where you flower?
in the radiant galleries
of what river, what fountain?
Your sanctuary is a grotto of colors.
Brilliant tongue
which speaks in private
to the eye and the ear.
Alone in what plant, water, dust, you go
clothed in wings of a dove
strewn with freshness and alert.
In your blue hair ride sweet odors.
Solitude turned elemental.

II

Crystalline riches, coined clouds,
remembering water from a height,
over the forests and meadows
you travel with your knapsacks of freshness
packed at once by groves
and grasses, clouds and cattle.
With your wet feet
innocently treading barefoot
you point your presence
made wholly first and last of tears.
Water of celestial solitudes.
Your fish are your minor angels
who water over everlasting treasures
in your frozen keeps.

III

Doncel de soledad, oh lirio armado
por azules espadas defendido,
gran señor con tu vara de fragancia,
a los cuentos del aire das oído.
A tu fiesta de nieve convidado
el insecto aturdido de distancia
licor de cielo escancia,
maestro de embriagueces
solitarias a veces.
Mayúscula inicial de la blancura:
De retazos de nube y agua pura
está urdido su cándido atavío
donde esplenden, nacidos de la altura
huevecillos celestes de rocío.

IV

Sueñas, magnolia casta, en ser paloma
o nubecilla enana, suspendida
sobre las hojas, luna fragmentada.
Solitaria inocencia recogida
en un nimbo de aroma.
Santa de la blancura inmaculada.
Soledad congelada
hasta ser alabastro
tumbal, lámpara o astro.
Tu oronda frente que la luz ampara
es del candor del mundo la alquitara
donde esencia secreta extrae el cielo.
En nido de hojas que el verdor prepara,
esperas resignada el don del vuelo.

III

Solitary young man, oh armored lily,
defended by blue swords,
great lord with your fragrant wand,
lend an ear to these winds' tales.
Bidden to your snow feast
the sipping insect dazed with distance
sky-bred reveals himself
drunken and at times alone.
Start with a blank anesthesia:
from whiffs of cloud and clear water
we weave our candid attire
where shine, borne from above
heavenly beads of dew.

IV

You dream, chaste flower, of being a dove
or a small cloud, hanging
above the leaves, to a shredded moon.
Solitary innocence gathered into
a basket of smells,
sainthood of immaculate whiteness.
A solitude frozen
till it turns to the alabaster
of tombs, a lamp or a star.
Your great brow suffused in light
is the world's candor, is the still
from which a secret essence comes to us from the sky.
In a nest of green leaves
resigned you await the gift of flight.

V

Flor de amor, flor de ángel, flor de abeja,
cuerpecillos medrosos, virginales
con pies de sombra, amortajados vivos,
ángeles en pañales.
El rostro de la dalia tras su reja,
los nardos que arden en su albura, altivos,
los jacintos cautivos
en su torre delgada
de aromas fabricada,
girasoles, del oro buscadores:
lenguas de soledad, todas las flores
niegan o asienten según habla el viento
y en la alquimia fugaz de los olores
preparan su fragante acabamiento.

VI

¡De murallas que viste el agua pura
y de cúpula de aves coronado
mundo de alas, prisión de transparencia
donde vivo encerrado!
Quiere entrar la verdura
por la ventana a pasos de paciencia,
y anuncias tu presencia
con tu cesta de frutas, lejanía.
Mas, cumplo cada día,
Capitán del color, antiguo amigo
de la tierra, mi límpido castigo.
Soy a la vez cautivo y carcelero
de esta celda de cal que anda conmigo,
de la que, oh muerte, guardas el llavero.

—*Jorge Carrera Andrade*

V

Flower of love, angel flower, bee's flower,
small bodies, virginal
with shadowy feet, dead alive,
angels in swaddling clothes.
The face of a dahlia behind her screen,
spikenard burning in her whiteness, haughty,
the captive hyacinths
in their slender tower
of sweet odors,
sunflowers, prospectors for gold:
solitude tasters, all the flowers
denying or affirming the speech of the winds
and in the fleeting alchemy of senses
who prepare their fragrant ends.

VI

Of walls attired in purest water
crowned by a dome of birds
whom their wings contain, lucent prison
where I live enclosed:
Greenness would enter by the window
with patient footsteps,
when you announce your presence
with your basket of fruits, remoteness.
But, I bear each day,
Color bearer, my old friend
here on earth, my own clear punishment.
I am at once prisoner and jailer
of this lime cell that goes about with me,
of which friend death you have the key.

CONVERSACIÓN A MI PADRE

Claro que ya lo sabes
que ya lo sabes todo
todo lo sabes claro.
Por eso también sabes
que tengo ganas de contártelo,
porque mientras lo cuento lo recuerdo
y así juntos los dos lo recordamos:
y yo escribiendo
y tú en silencio a mi lado.

. . . Pues desde que te fuiste
han sucedido tantas cosas . . .
La gente muere y nace,
se enferma, convalece,
se pone bien, ya come
su poquito de sopa y su pescado,
se levanta, y al sol
como los gatos junto a la ventana.
Otros no se levantan
y se quedan tendidos
y se mueren.
Se mueren como tú,
como los otros y las otras
y todos los que te siguieron
y los que seguirán siguiéndote.
Aunque también la gente vive.
Sigue viviendo, a pesar de los llantos y los lutos.
Y un día le dan ganas
de salir de paseo, de ir al cine,
de tocar al piano lo que a ti te gustaba.
Y no es que así te entierre más;

CONVERSATION WITH MY FATHER

Clearly you already know it
you already know it all
know it all clearly.
Because of this you know too
how I wish to tell it,
for while I speak I am recalling
as I sit here beside you:
I writing
and you silent beside me.

. . . Well, since you left
many things have happened . . .
Men have died and been born,
grown ill and recovered,
felt well, taken their
sup of soup, piece of fish,
got up, gone into the sun
like cats to the window.
Others do not get up
but remain stretched out
and die.
Die like you,
and others, men and women,
and all that you love
and all those who follow you.
Although many still live.
They keep living, despite weeping and mourning.
And one day they want to go
for a walk, to go to the movies,
to play the piano much as you do.
Not that in this way I bury you deeper;

es que, viviendo más, más te recuerda.
Porque vive contigo, con lo que tú querías,
con tus libros. (Aún tengo,
en su cubierta gris, *Peñas arriba*,
que te dejaste abierta
aquel día . . .)
Y seguimos viviendo todos
y ya ves, recordándote todos los días.
Y decimos: este postre le gustaba,
y caminaba así, porque siempre iba aprisa,
y una vez se afeitó el bigote
y se lo volvió a dejar en seguida.
. . . .

Tantas veces he pensado
en lo que te gustaría
eso de andar por estos barrios, de ir al Museo
y allí contarme cómo son *Las Meninas*
y luego mirar juntos *La Duquesa de Alba*,
aquella doña Cayetana de Silva
que tu hermano Pepe una vez trajo
desde la otra orilla.
Sí que fuera bonito
recorrer tantas salas—menos las cositas
francesas del dieciocho tan tontas,
y las inglesas con sus carnes de mantequilla—.
Y luego salir al parque
y sentarnos a conversar sin prisas
y mirar cómo el aire del ocaso
va moviendo las aguas del estanque encendidas.

Ya sabes cómo llegó la guerra
y cómo en ella la gente se moría;

but that, more living, they remember you more.
Because they live with you, with what you enjoyed
in your books. (Though I still
have in its grey covers, *Peñas arriba*,
which you left open
that day . . .)
And we all continue living
and you see, remembering you daily.
And we say: he liked this dessert,
and used to walk here, always in a hurry,
and once shaved off his moustache
and at once let it grow again.
. . . .

More than once I thought
how much you enjoyed
walking in these parts, to go to the museum
and there tell me about *Las Meninas*
and then gazing side by side at *La Duquesa de Alba*,
that Doña Cayetana de Silva
that your brother Pepe once brought
from the other side.
Yes, it would be fine
to wander again through so many rooms—except
the little French things of the 18th century, so silly,
and the English women with their buttery flesh.
And then go into the park
and sit down to talk at our ease
observing how at sunset the air
moves rippling the lighted waters of the pool.

You already know how the war came about
and how in it people died;

y cómo terminó la guerra
y cómo sigue la gente con su manía
de destruirse, de matarse
como si no fuera poca toda la carne dividida.
Y que no escarmentamos.
Y es tan triste pensar que toda esta agonía
pudiera desaparecer sencillamente
con que aprendiera el hombre a entregar su sonrisa,
y a decir una palabra buena, de verdad,
y a querer, de verdad, ennoblecer la vida.
Pero no quiere, ya lo ves.
Lo que quiere es que siga
esta danza tremenda de la muerte
que no es la muerte tuya y mía
—es decir, la de andar por casa,
la que se recibe en zapatillas
o cuando más en el campo abierto
o en el agua limpia—,
sino la otra, la muerte a montones
en los campos cerrados y las aguas pestíferas,
la mala muerte que baja del aire
y que sale de donde estaba escondida
para aplastar los cuerpos como nueces
y segar las cabezas como espigas.

Y luego hay otras cosas:
porque hay eso de la bomba atómica,
que a mí, entre nosotros, no me da frío ni calor
—hasta el día en que me deje frío para siempre.
Y eso sería lo de menos.
Lo de más será que nos quedemos ciegos o deformes
y no podamos ver un día la luz del sol
no tomar en los dedos una rosa

and how the war ended
and how the people's mania followed it
bent on destruction, killing
as if all the maceration of flesh were not enough.
And we learn nothing.
And it is sad to think that all this agony
could simply disappear
if man could learn to wipe the grin from his face,
and to say one good word, truly,
and wish, in fact, to make life noble.
But he does not want it, as you see.
What he wants is to follow
this overwhelming dance of death
which is not your death nor mine
—that is to say, death as it may happen
about the house, one that is met in slippers
or at most in the open country
or in clear water,
without the other, heaped up mountainous
in stinking fields and foul waters,
death which drops from the air
and comes from hiding
to crush bodies as if they were nuts
reap them as if they were heads of wheat.

Then there are other things:
the case of the atomic bomb,
to me, among ourselves, leaves me neither hot nor cold
—to the day it leaves me in eternity cold.
And that would be the last of my worries.
That which worries me most is to be blinded or maimed
unable to see a day full of sunlight
nor hold a rose in my fingers

porque los ojos estén caídos en un pozo de nieblas
y los dedos se nos hayan quedado secos como la estopa.
Digo que, si lo vamos a ver, casi no me importa.
Pero la inquisición de tener que sentarnos
en esas sillas de metal o de qué se yo qué jerigonza,
con espejos y cristales donde no deben estar,
que es en las paredes y en las ventanas,
sino espejos donde se ponen los platos y las copas,
y cristales en las mesas en lugar de madera,
para tener que estarles mirando las faldas a las señoras,
esa sí que es inquisición peor que la de la bomba.
Cuando tú te fuiste apenas empezaba todo eso,
pero lo que es ahora . . .
Te digo que me dan ganas de meterme en una casa vieja
con cortinas y alfombras
(pero de las de verdad, no estas de celanese y seda
    sintética)
y butacas anchas y cómodas
(para no tener que estar sentado como de compromiso
con tubos de metal que nos pinchan las corvas)
y lámparas como las que gracias a Dios tengo yo en casa
(y no de esas otras
que están lo mismo en las funerarias
que en los salones de los hoteles, lámparas sordas
que alumbran, sí, pero que no dan sombra.)
Y lo peor es que eso le gusta a la gente,
y hay quien destroza
toda una chimenea de mármol que tiene en la sala de su
    casa
para poner en su lugar un artefacto idiota
con termostato y regulador de aire y qué sé yo,
pero en el que, como no hay llamas no hay color
y como no hay color no hay luz

for the eyes have fallen into a pit of darkness
the fingers remain dried up like burlap.
I say, that if we are to see, it means almost nothing to me.
But the inquisition of having to be seated
in those metal chairs or made of I don't know what,
with glass mirrors where you may not sit
which are on the walls and the window,
but mirrors where plates and cups are set
and glassware on the tables instead of wood,
so that you have to keep looking at the skirts of the ladies,
that yes, is more an inquisition than the bomb.
When you left, all of this had hardly begun,
but now . . .
I tell you I yearn to go into an old curtained house
with rugs on the floors
(but real ones, not those made of wood-fiber and synthetic
    silk)
and wide comfortable chairs
(so as not to be seated as if out of courtesy
on hollow metal stuck into our hams)
and lamps like those which thank God
I have at home
(and like those others
found in funeral parlors
or hotel lobbies, lamps, yes, which give light
but cast no shadow).
And the worst is that it pleases people to have it
this way, and there are those
who tear up a whole marble fireplace in their homes
to replace it with an idiotic artifact
embodying a thermostat and air control and
I don't know what else,
but which, since there is no visible flame,

y como no hay luz tampoco hay sombra,
sombra para entornar los ojos
y dejar de leer al doblar la hoja,
y sombra de abrir los ojos
y acostumbrar la vista temblorosa
y ponerla otra vez en la palabra
que nos espera al terminar la estrofa.
(Con todo esto, padre mío,
dirás que me estoy poniendo viejo;
y tendrás razón.
Ya a mis años prefiero
llegar a casa y colgar el abrigo y el sombrero,
y beber una taza de té con limón
o el chocolate junto a la ventana.
Como gracias a Dios no tengo frío,
tranquilamente dejo
que haga el gato lo que le dé la gana.
Y si eso del frío y del gato
nada tiene que ver,
la cuestión es pasar el rato
tú y yo y el que me quiera leer.)

Y vamos a otra cosa.
Tú bien estás, creo yo, allá arriba.
¿Fuiste por fin a tu tierra de Castilla
como pensé yo que harías?
De seguro que te habrá gustado
encontrarte con tantas gentes amigas
y ponerte con ellas a conversar
en una era de Cubas el mediodía.
(Habrá quien se figure que esto es una errata,
porque no sabe del pueblocito que tú querías;
a donde, como yo pueda, habrán de ir

gives off heat without light
and since there is no light there are no shadows
shadows for the half closing of the eyes
to quit reading and turning the page,
to quit reading with half vision
shadows to redirect the wavering eyes
and refocus them on the word
which awaits us at the end of the strophe.
(With all this, father,
you will say that I am growing old;
and you'll be right.
At my years I prefer
to go home and hang up my overcoat and hat,
and to take a cup of tea with lemon in it
or chocolate beside the window.
Since thank God I am not cold,
I tranquilly allow the cat
to do whatever he pleases.
And if the question of a cat hot or cold
is beside the point,
the question for us, you and me, and whoever else
is to pass the time reading.)

Let us turn to other things,
in my opinion, you are well off up there.
Did you finally go to your own Castilian land
as I thought you would?
You must have enjoyed meeting
so many friends
and stopped to talk with them
on some Cuban threshing floor at midday.
(There will be those who will think this an error
for they do not know of the little town that you loved;

a volver a su suelo tus cenizas.)
Pero vamos a hablar de otras cosas,
¿verdad? Cómo te divertiría
ver que tu hijo el poeta se ha metido a pintor
—claro que para no hacer más que tonterías—.
Es que, como bien tú lo sabes
—ahora me acuerdo de aquellas montañas verdecitas
y de aquellos cielos azules que pintabas al temple
para los Nacimientos que en Port-Bou nos hacías—
digo que, como sabes,
es una cosas muy entretenida
eso de embadurnar un lienzo con colores
sin saber si te va a salir una flor o un gorila.
A mí hasta ahora más me salen los monstruos,
pero me queda la esperanza de que algún día . . .

Y con esa esperanza te dejo por ahora.
Es tarde. No te dejo, ya lo sabes;
que con dejar de hablarte no te dejo,
que me voy, pero sigo escuchándote,
que estoy contigo, aunque te deje . . .
Quiero decir . . . que no me voy, vaya;
pero que voy a terminar esta carta,
aunque me quede a tu lado siempre.
Porque dejo de hablarte, pero te sigo hablando.
En fin, que me he hecho un lío, pero tú me comprendes.

—*Eugenio Florit*

where, as soon as I can, will go his ashes.)
But to change the subject,
you would be amused
to see how your son
the poet has turned painter
—of course only to put down mere nonsense.
Because, as you well know
—now I recall those little green mountains
and those blue skies that you painted in tempera
for the Nativity scenes you made for us at Port-Bou—
I say, as you know,
it is something very amusing
to daub a canvas with paint
without knowing whether it is going to be flowers or a
     gorilla.
With me it is mostly monsters
but I hope some day . . .

And with this hope I leave you for the time being.
It is late. You know I never leave you;
that to stop talking is not to quit you,
I take myself off, but still listening,
I am with you when I leave you . . .
I mean . . . that I do not go, leaving;
but let me finish this letter
though I am seated beside you forever.
For when I stop talking to you, I continue to talk.
Well, I am making a botch of it, but you
          understand.

POR MI VENTANA

¡Mira, mira como vuelan!
Son las hojas destacadas
   del inexorable Otoño.
No hay porqué aflijirse
     ellas volverán
   en la radiante Primavera.

¡Ay de mí! las ilusiones
   perdidas
son hojas caídas del arbol
   del corazón
    esas no volverán,
Muertas están en el Ibierno
   de la vida humana.

—*Raquel Hélène Rose Hoheb Williams*

FROM MY WINDOW

Look, look how they fall
They are the dried leaves
     of the inexorable Autumn
No need to be sorrowful
        they will relive
     in the radiant Springtime.

Alas, for lost illusions
they are leaves falling from
     the tree of the heart
     these will not relive
But they are dead in the
     Winter of human life.

AL POETA WILLIAM CARLOS WILLIAMS

En él estaba contenida
la enramada.

Era su voluntad,

una entrada
en los claros designios
de las aguas.

Los sonidos del cielo
se oían con su oído.

(Cuando Dios hizo un ruido
que no probó la luna,
ni se aclaró en el viento,

el creyó que llegaban
los rumores del alba,

y es que oyó que el silencio
de Dios se sosegaba.)

Cuando lo vi
rodeado de la tarde,

—rostro de isla,
longitud de aire—,

cuando llegué hasta él
desde mí misma,

TO W.C.W.

The whole arbor
is contained in him.

It is his will,

an entrance
to the clear design
of the waters.

Heavenly music
wakes in his ear.

(When God stirred,
the moon never varied
nor the wind,

a rumor
of approaching dawn,

stillness become
God's silence.)

When I saw him
of an afternoon

—an island face
in the air—

when I came upon him
from within,

la espiga que era niña
vertió su corazón:

lo dio al agua de abril,
a la sombra de mayo,
lo dio al ardiente paso del verano.

El ruiseñor yacente
soñó con el laurel,

y el laurel
con el ciervo transparente.

Y el mundo que era un ojo
cerrado a la cadencia
del ala, de la piedra, del torrente,

se abrió, miró su forma,
amó su imagen viva para siempre.

Vio que era bueno
porque en sí tenía,
el ámbito del vuelo.

—*Eunice Odio*

the sprouting wheat
poured from his heart:

it was April
to embowered May,

the transience of
summer quieted.

The nightingale at ease
dreams of the laurel,

and the laurel
of the all-seeing heart.

The world is an ear shut
to the cadence of
wing, stone and torrent,

gazed upon its shape,
eternally loved
its living image.

Saw that it was good
because in it was held
the boundaries of flight.

Williams on Spanish

These statements, which range from autobiographical references to literary pronouncements, further illuminate Williams's relationship to Spanish, not only in translation but in its fundamental importance to him.

I had a scrap with a conductor at five this morning on the way from Madrid to Cordova; he insisted on making me pay double for a fare I had no ticket for. . . . You should have heard me slinging choice Rutherford Spanish at him with that peculiar Hackensack accent which you know so well.　　—Letter to Floss, 1910*

I'm going to begin work on a translation from the Spanish in another month. The work is from Herrera, a lyric poet and a contemporary of Shakespeare's. He has never been done into English but is nevertheless one of the world's masters as Pound assures me. . . . No kind of practice is better than just such translating work.　　—Letter to brother Edgar, 1910

Take the trouble to send me the names of the Spaniards you spoke of in a former letter, also addresses and the names of a couple of worthwhile spanish books—modern poetry. Please do not forget this as I am now in a position to do a little work along this horizontal.　　—Letter to Ezra Pound, 1921

*WCW papers, Lilly Library, Indiana University Bloomington.

If more of the Spanish were better translated—more in the spirit of modern American letters, . . . our efforts away from vaguely derived, nostalgic effects so deleterious to the mind would be replaced by the directness and objectivity we so painfully seek.

—"Lorca and the Tradition of Spanish Poetry,"
draft, 1938*

Góngora was the man! . . . a lyric poet [who] brought the new adventure to its fullest fruition . . . and beyond it—to amazing effect. Góngora is the only Spanish poet whose inventions, at the beginning of the 17th century, retain a lively interest for us today.

—"Federico García Lorca," *Kenyon Review,* 1939

What influence can Spanish have on us who speak a derivative of English in North America? To shake us free for a reconsideration of the poetic line. . . . It looks as though our salvation may come not from within ourselves but from the outside.

—Lecture at Inter-American Writers' Conference,
Puerto Rico, 1941

I thought Spanish was a good language. . . . We've dropped it in our day, curiously enough, but my parents spoke Spanish, preferably to English, and my brother and I heard it and understood it because they said things in Spanish that they didn't want us to understand. So I liked Spanish.

—Interview with John W. Gerber, 1950

I have always wanted to do some translations from the Spanish. It was my mother's native language. . . . [It] has a strong appeal for me, temperamentally, as a relief from the classic mood of both French and Italian. . . . It has a place of its own, an independent place very sympathetic to the New World.

—*The Autobiography of William Carlos Williams,* 1951

* WCW papers, Poetry Collection, University at Buffalo, State University of New York.

Ezra found an old copy of lyrical poems, out of Spanish Romantic Literature, and knowing that Spanish was spoken in my home, gave them to me. . . . I began to translate some of them, working on and off for a year, finding it difficult but fascinating. . . . I've always determined to go back to it someday; Spanish still seems to me synonymous with romantic.

—*I Wanted to Write a Poem*, 1958

My father spoke Spanish quite as easily as he spoke English. . . . Spanish was the language spoken in the household. . . . So that as children my brother and I heard Spanish constantly spoken about us. A steady flow of West Indians, South Americans, and other speakers of the Spanish language came to visit us.

—*Yes, Mrs. Williams*, 1959

Annotations

Abbreviations used in these notes:

ACLAP   *Anthology of Contemporary Latin-American Poetry*,
ed. Dudley Fitts (New Directions, 1942; see TSAP)

BLOOMINGTON   The Williams archive at the Lilly Library,
Indiana University Bloomington

BUFFALO   The Williams archive at the Poetry Collection, Univer-
sity at Buffalo, State University of New York

C   *The Correspondence of William Carlos Williams &*
Louis Zukofsky, ed. Barry Ahearn (Wesleyan, 2003)

CPI   *The Collected Poems of William Carlos Williams,*
Volume I: 1909–1939, ed. A. Walton Litz and
Christopher MacGowan (New Directions, 1986)

CPII   *The Collected Poems of William Carlos Williams,*
Volume II: 1939–1962, ed. Christopher MacGowan
(New Directions, 1988)

E   E-mail correspondence with editor Jonathan Cohen

ER   *Evergreen Review* (Winter 1959; "The Eye of Mexico")

HR   *The Hudson Review* (Spring 2011)

JVA   José Vázquez-Amaral (1913–1987; Mexican-born
critic and translator of U.S. poetry, including Pound's
Cantos; founding chairman of Rutgers's Department
of Spanish and Portuguese)

MA   *El mono azul* (1936–1939; weekly paper published in
Madrid by the Alianza de Intelectuales Antifascistas
para la Defensa de la Cultura)

NWW   *New World Writing* (Dec. 1958; "New Writing from
Latin America")

O   *Others* (Aug. 1916; "Spanish-American Number";
featuring the work of seven poets, two of whom are
not represented in the present collection, i.e., Leopold
Díaz and Juan Julián Lastra)

PSC   *Poesías selectas castellanas* ("Choice Spanish Poetry"),
          ed. Manuel Josef Quintina (Gomez Fuentenebro,
          1817; second volume of four-volume set, given WCW
          by Pound)

SS   . . . *And Spain Sings: Fifty Loyalist Ballads Adapted
          by American Poets*, ed. M. J. Benardete and Rolfe
          Humphries (Vanguard, 1937)

TSAP   *12 Spanish American Poets*, ed. H. R. Hays (Yale,
          1943; Hays produced the bio-critical notes for ACLAP)

WGW   William George Williams (1851–1918; father of
          WCW; born in England, grew up in the West Indies,
          was fluent in Spanish, traveled widely in Latin Amer-
          ica as businessman)

YALE   The Williams archive at the Beinecke Rare Book and
          Manuscript Library, Yale University

OTHERS / 1916

RAFAEL ARÉVALO MARTÍNEZ; Guatemala, 1884–1975. Poet, short-story writer, novelist, diplomat, director of Guatemala's national library for two decades. Although he published several books of poetry during his lifetime, the best of which is widely considered to be *Las rosas de Engaddi* (Sánchez & de Guise, 1923; "The Roses of Engaddi"), he is remembered more for his fiction, in particular his "psychozoological" short stories. ACLAP notes: "His verse is vigorous and flexible, and his hard-bitten style frequently makes the matter-of-fact seem wild and strange."

"Fragments of 'Las Imposibles'": Published in O. From Arévalo Martínez's *Los atormentados* (Gutiérrez, 1914; "The Tormented"). Translated in collaboration with WGW.

The poem's title echoes the famous proverb attributed to French statesman Chrétien Guillaume de Lamoignon de Malesherbes (1721–1794), which established itself in Spanish as follows: "Haríamos muchas más cosas si creyéramos que son muchas menos las imposibles" [We'll do many more things if we believe there are many less impossible things].

"My Life Is a Memory": Published in O. From Arévalo Martínez's *Los atormentados*. Translated in collaboration with WGW.

"The Sensation of a Smell": Published in O. From Arévalo Martínez's *Los atormentados*. Translated in collaboration with WGW.

Arévalo Martínez's most famous work of fiction is his psycho-zoological tale, "El hombre que parecía un caballo" ("The Man Who Resembled a Horse"), published in 1915. This story has been called the most famous Latin American short story of the twentieth century. WCW translated it with the help of WGW, and published it in *The Little Review* (Dec. 1918). His translation later appeared in *New Directions 1944*, "the annual exhibition gallery of divergent literary trends published by New Directions."

WCW used the following passage from this story—in Spanish only—for the epigraph of his 1917 collection of poems, *Al Que Quiere!* ("To Him Who Wants It"):

> Había sido un arbusto desmedrado que prolonga sus filamentos hasta encontrar el humus necesario en una tierra nueva. ¡Y cómo me nutría! Me nutría con la beatitud con que las hojas trémulas de clorofila se extienden al sol; con la beatitud con que una raíz encuentra un cadáver en descomposición; con la beatitud con que los convalecientes dan sus pasos vacilantes en las mañanas de primavera, bañadas de luz; . . . [Quote in book had five typos that enraged WGW.]

Here is WCW's translation as it appears in the published story:

> I had been an adventurous shrub which prolongs its filaments until it finds the necessary humus in new earth. And how I fed! I fed with the joy of tremulous leaves of chlorophyll that spread themselves to the sun; with the joy with which a root encounters a decomposing corpse; with the joy with which convalescents take their vacillating steps in the light-flooded mornings of spring; . . .

Following the story in the New Directions anthology, WCW's note on the translation describes his collaboration with WGW, who "was accomplished in two languages, Spanish and English," and who for business "did a lot of travelling especially in South and Central America [sometimes for months on end]."

JOSÉ SANTOS CHOCANO; Peru, 1875–1934. Poet, revolutionary, journalist, diplomat. Inspired by Whitman, he was known as "The Singer of America" because of the first line of his famous poem, "Coat of Arms": "I am the singer of America, native and wild: / my lyre has a soul, my song a dream." He wrote epic and lyric poems. He was a prominent leader of Latin American modernism, and celebrated for his poetry that synthesizes the history, culture, and landscape of his America. He proudly initiated the movement called *mundonovismo*, or New Worldism.

"The Song of the Road": Published in O. From Santos Chocano's *¡Fiat lux!* (Ollendorff, 1908; "Let There Be Light!"). Translated in collaboration with WGW.

Comparison of the Williams translation with the one made by John Pierrepont Rice demonstrates modernist versus Victorian translation poetics. Rice's translation, titled "A Song of the Road," was published in *Poetry* (Feb. 1918). Here are the opening stanzas:

> The way was black,
> The night was mad with lightning; I bestrode
> My wild young colt upon a mountain road.
> And, crunching onward, like a monster's jaws
> His ringing hoof-beats their glad rhythm kept;
> Breaking the glassy surface of the pools
> Where hidden waters slept.
> A million buzzing insects in the air
> On droning wing made sullen discord there.
>
> But suddenly, afar, beyond the wood,
> Beyond the dark pall of my brooding thought,
> I saw lights cluster like a swarm of wasps
> Among the branches caught.
> "The inn!" I cried, and on his living flesh
> My broncho felt the lash and neighed with eagerness.

And all this time the cool and quiet wood
Uttered no sound, as though it understood.

Until there came to me upon the night
A voice so clear, so clear, so ringing sweet!—
A voice as of a woman, and her song
Dropped like soft music winging at my feet,
And seemed a sigh that, with my spirit blending,
Lengthened and lengthened out, and had no ending.

Rice (1879–1941), a professor of Romance languages, followed the conventional approach of his day to verse translation, as seen for instance in his imposition of English metrics, end rhymes, inversions, and archaisms.

ALFONSO GUILLÉN ZELAYA; Honduras, 1888–1947. Poet, journalist, diplomat, philosopher. He is considered the first Honduran of note to write social-conscience poetry. During the years of the First World War, while living in New York in the diplomatic service of his country, he was an editor of the bilingual magazine, *Pan American Poetry*, dedicated to furthering the cause of Pan-Americanism. José Santos Chocano called him "a clear spring flowing from virgin soil, shaded by trees of home, virtuous with the deep spiritual nature of Latin Americans."

"Lord, I Ask a Garden": Published in O. Presumably from the manuscript; of Guillén Zelaya's *El agua de la fuente* (no record of publication; "Water from the Spring"); text here from his *El quinto silencio* (Universidad Nacional Autónoma de Honduras, 1994; "The Fifth Silence"). Translated in collaboration with WGW.

The translation also appears in Thomas Walsh's *Hispanic Anthology* (1920), which says about Guillén Zelaya: "His principal poetic works are contained in *El agua de la fuente* about to appear and *De la luz ignorada* ["Of Unknown Light"] (in preparation)." A 1920 issue of *Boletín de la Real Academia Española* cites the book, *El agua de la fuente*, as if published.

The "Manifesto" published in O ("Spanish-American Number") contains, in part, the following information about the poet and his relationship with the magazine:

> *Not long ago, Alfonso Guillén Zelaya, of Honduras, materialized in New York, and the Quijotian dream quickly evolved of bartering the product of men and women who appear in* OTHERS *with that of men and women of Spanish America; and so, translations from* OTHERS *will be used in Spanish American periodicals; in fact it is planned to have a Spanish edition of* OTHERS *under the title,* OTROS! *In this instance, the advice of Señor Zelaya has been invaluable.*

These statements were written by Alfred Kreymborg, the magazine's editor, with likely input from WCW, an associate editor. It is thought that WCW was the driving force behind this issue.

LUIS CARLOS LÓPEZ; Colombia, 1879–1950. Poet, diplomat, businessman. Nicknamed *El Tuerto* (One-Eye), though actually he was cross-eyed, he is famous for his caricatures in verse of the provincial society of his hometown, Cartagena, where he spent practically his entire life. He served briefly as consul in Munich (1928) and Baltimore (1937). His poetic world is full of parody, irony, satire, and antipoetry. He is considered one of the most important Colombian poets of the twentieth century, and among the best regional writers in Latin American literature.

"Verses to the Moon": Published in O. From Carlos López's *Posturas difíciles* (Pueyo, 1909; "Awkward Positions"). Translated in collaboration with WGW.

JOSÉ ASUNCIÓN SILVA; Colombia, 1865–1896. Poet, novelist, diplomat, businessman. A misanthropic dandy, he produced a limited but influential body of work during his short lifetime, for which he is recognized as one of the founders of Latin American modernism. He modeled his poetics on that of Poe, as well as on

French symbolism (in Europe he socialized with Mallarmé and Verlaine). His melancholy lyricism was something new in Latin America. Following great personal losses, he committed suicide. He is still revered as a cultural icon in his homeland.

"The Disease of the Century": Published in O. From Silva's *Poesías* (Maucci, 1908; "Poems"). Translated in collaboration with WGW.

AND SPAIN SINGS / 1930s

LUPERCIO (LEONARDO) DE ARGENSOLA; Spain, 1559–1613. Poet, historian, playwright. The king of Spain appointed him chief chronicler of the crown of Aragon. His dramas are praised by Cervantes in *Don Quixote*. But his lasting reputation as a writer rests on his lyric poems. While at Naples he destroyed all those within his reach, so that what remains are only the pieces that happened to be in the hands of friends. They were collected and published, together with the poems of his equally celebrated brother Bartholome, by Lupercio's son.

"Cancion": Published in *Adam & Eve & the City* (Alcestis Press, 1936) and in CPI. From the first stanza of de Argensola's "Canción" ("Song"); WCW used the Spanish text in PSC.

WCW told Louis Zukofsky in a letter (30? Oct. 1935), in which he sent this translation: "Note: the third line of the Spanish is particularly fine" (C). About this same line, in notes to himself for his essay on Lorca and Spanish poetry (see *Kenyon Review*, Spring 1939), WCW says: "an amazingly Spanish line, with all the harshness of the language at its most attached indigenousness" (BUFFALO).

Here is the complete first stanza of the poem, which contains a total of six stanzas:

> Alivia sus fatigas
> El labrador cansado,
> Quando [*sic*] su yerta barba escarcha cubre,
> Pensando en las espigas
> Del Agosto abrasado,
> Y en los lagares ricos del Octubre:
> La hoz se le descubre
> Quando el arado apaña,
> Y con dulces memorias le acompaña.

My translation of the closing three lines, which WCW did not translate, is: "The sickle catches his eye / As he mends the plow, / Working on it with sweet memories now" (JC).

ANONYMOUS ROMANCEROS; Spain. The authors of Spanish *romances*—ballads—are known as *romanceros*. Their poems survived centuries in the oral tradition, and they link medieval heroic epic to modern poetry. Traditionally, they treated frontier episodes, history as it happened, and also lyrical themes. They were compressed dramatic narratives that originally were sung to a tune. The heroic style of these balladeers inspired the political *romances* of the Spanish Civil War, which exerted a tremendous force as the rallying cry of the people of Spain.

"Tears That Still Lacked Power": Published in *Adam & Eve & the City* and in CPI. WCW used the Spanish text in PSC.

"Poplars of the Meadow": Published in *Adam & Eve & the City* and in CPI. WCW used the Spanish text in PSC.

WCW published the following early translation of this *romance* in his 1913 collection, *The Tempers* (he dedicated this book to Carlos Hoheb, his late maternal uncle):

Poplars of the meadow,
Fountains of Madrid,
Now I am absent from you
All are slandering me.

Each of you is telling
How evil my chance is
The wind among the branches,
The fountains in their welling
To every one telling
You were happy to see.
Now I am absent from you
All are slandering me.

With good right I may wonder
For that at my last leaving
The plants with sighs heaving
And the waters in tears were.
That you played double, never
Thought I this could be,
Now I am absent from you
All are slandering me.

There full in your presence
Music you sought to waken,
Later I'm forsaken
Since you are ware of my absence.
God, wilt Thou give me patience
Here while suffer I ye,
Now I am absent from you
All are slandering me.

Comparison of the two versions reveals WCW's development as a
poet toward a "more concrete and controlled style" (Debby Rosen-
thal, "'Accurate Equivalents': Comparing Williams's 1913 and
1936 'Translations from the Spanish,'" *William Carlos Williams
Review* 16.1 [Spring 1990]: 30–35). The later version also demon-
strates WCW's commitment to using the American idiom.

FRANCISCO DE QUEVEDO; Spain, 1580–1645. Nobleman, politician, writer. Along with his lifelong rival, Luis de Góngora, he was one of the most prominent poets of the Baroque era, known as the Golden Age of Spanish literature. Many consider him the greatest of that period. His poetry, full of puns and elaborate conceits, uses precise, economic, rational language, with complex ideas presented in a simple and succinct style. Góngora's work, in stark contrast, is characterized by an ornate, esoteric style, full of metaphor, classical allusions, neologisms, and syntactic complexity.

The two fragments here are from WCW's unpublished essay (YALE) that he wrote to accompany his translation of what he thought was Quevedo's novella, *El perro y la calentura* (1625; *The Dog and the Fever*, translated with his mother in the 1930s, and published in 1954 by Shoe String Press). Both represent the Spaniard's brilliant satiric verse using popular oral forms. Source of Spanish texts WCW used is unknown; texts here are from Quevedo's *Colección de poesías escogidas* (Imprenta Real, 1795; "Selected Poems").

The first fragment comes from one of his *letrillas* (poems with eight-syllable lines in short stanzas) whose refrain is: "Ello dirá, / Y si no, / Lo diré yo" (Time will tell, / And if not, / I will tell you). WCW rendered lines 3 and 4 of the opening quatrain, which begins: "Oyente, si tú me ayudas / Con tu malicia y tu risa" (Listener, if you help me / With your backbiting and your laugh). The second fragment is the opening quatrain of one of Quevedo's *romances*, written, as WCW notes, in response to polemics against him from the pulpit.

About the following three *romances* from the Spanish Civil War, WCW told Zukofsky in a letter (6 May 1937): "I've been translating Spanish revolutionary ballads." And in another letter to Zukofsky sent the next day, he said: "My translations keep as close as possible to the pace and meter of the Spanish. I have done them line for line and almost word for word" (C).

MIGUEL HERNÁNDEZ; Spain, 1910–1942. Poet, playwright. A goatherd in his youth, he joined the Communist Party in 1936 and fought in the Spanish Civil War. His wartime *romances* are among the most famous. His verse written before the war was complex and Góngoristic in style, and then became more intimate, simple, and full of *duende* (deep soul). His best work is at once tragic and lyric. Caught by the Nationalists after the war, he was condemned to death, but his sentence was commuted to life after international protests. He died in prison soon afterward.

"Wind of the Village": Published in CPII. First published in SS; translation made at the request of editors Benardete and Humphries, who provided the Spanish text and a "rough translation" by Benardete in "literal but rhythmical prose." From MA (24 Sept. 1936); later published in Hernández's first book of war poems, *Viento del pueblo* (Socorro Rojo, 1937; "Wind from the People").

Comparison of the rough translation at BUFFALO (presumably that by Benardete) and the finished rendering by WCW shows the process of his poetic effort to re-create the ballad. Here are the opening and closing verses of the former:

> Seated above the dead
> who are silent these two months
> I kiss empty shoes
> and furiously seize
> hand of the heart
> and the soul that supports it.
> Let my voice rise to the mountains
> and crash down to the earth in thunder.
> This my throat demands
> from this day and forever.
> Draw near to my clamor
> village of the same milk as I,
> tree that with your roots
> holds me imprisoned,

so that I am here to love you
and I am here to defend you
with my blood and with word of mouth
like two faithful rifles.

. . . .

I sing with the voice of a lute
my own village, for your heros [*sic*];
your anguish as my own,
your misfortunes that derive
from the same temper and weeping
and of the same timber
your thoughts and my own mien,
your heart beats and my blood,
your grief and my own celebrations.
Outer buttress of emptiness
seems this life to me.
I am here to live merely
while the soul lies sleeping,
and I am here to die
when my hour shall arrive,
in the very springs of the village
from now on for evermore.
We drink of life over and over
and death we gulp once only.

The translation of *pueblo* as village, in the poem's title and body,
represents one possibility of the word's meaning; another is peo-
ple, which in the light of Hernández's other work at the time is
more accurate. WCW uses both meanings. The reference to "the
voice of the lute" in the poem's closing lines contains a mistrans-
lation of *luto*, which means mourning, not lute (*laúd*).

RAFAEL BELTRÁN LOGROÑO; Spain. Poet, journalist. Lit-
tle is known about this Loyalist poet of the Spanish Civil War.
The same is true of most authors of the countless *romances* pub-
lished during the war—poets who had a poem or two printed, or
maybe more, and then after the war's end, as poets, they faded

into obscurity. It is known that he wrote for the magazine *Eco*, that he was wounded fighting in Catalonia in 1938, and that the following year a pamphlet of his *romances*, titled *Héroes* (Europa-América, 1939), was published in Madrid. He was, in fact, one of the war's most popular poets.

"Johnny of Laviana": Published in CPII. First published in SS; translation made at the request of editors Benardete and Humphries, who provided the Spanish text and a literal translation by Benardete (BUFFALO). From MA (1 Oct. 1936); later published in Beltrán Logroño's *Héroes*.

MARIANO DEL ALCÁZAR; Spain. Poet. Less is known about this *romancero* than about his comrade, Beltrán Logroño. We know only his name and this one poem. Juan Zaro suggests his name might be a pseudonym, chosen by one of the big-name poets, such as Rafael Alberti or Emilio Prados, to avoid an overwhelming presence in the paper where his *romance* was published (E). Further suggestive that his name is a fiction, it recalls the famous Siege of the Alcázar in Toledo, a highly symbolic Nationalist victory in the opening stages of the war.

"Juan Montoya": Published in CPII. First published in SS; translation made at the request of editors Benardete and Humphries, who provided the Spanish text and a literal translation by Benardete. From MA (1 Oct. 1936).

The poem's closing line in Spanish refers to a *civil*, which in Spain and also in the context of this poem is a civil guardsman (federal paramilitary police), not civilian. WCW's (mis)translation is likely based on the literal given him.

ANONYMOUS POET; Spain. Thought to be from the mountainous area of northern Spain along the border with France.

"A Pretty Girl": Handwritten footnote in typescript at BUFFALO. From Spanish text and translation in Salvador de Madariaga's essay, "Spanish Popular Poetry," *Shelley & Calderón and Other Essays on English and Spanish Poetry* (Constable, 1920).

WCW discovered this lyric during the course of his research for his essay on Lorca, "Federico García Lorca," published in *The Kenyon Review* (Spring 1939). WCW quotes the Spanish text in the essay, but provides no translation. However, in one of the many unpublished drafts of the essay, he includes his translation, which differs from de Madariaga's rendering that appears in "Spanish Popular Poetry":

> A pretty maid
> Leaned over her window.
> She asked for my soul,
> I gave her my heart,
> She asked for my soul,
> And I said farewell.

As for the source of this folk-song verse, de Madariaga says only that its author is anonymous and that it "may be heard in the high valleys of the Asturian Pyrenees."

SWEATED BLOOD / 1940 & '50s

LUIS PALÉS MATOS; Puerto Rico, 1898–1959. Poet, journalist. He is one of the great poets of the Afro-Antillean school. ACLAP notes: "Few writers of his school can compare with him in the grotesque blend of sensual and spiritual values which he creates—a blend which never lapses into pure burlesque, and which is always saved from vulgarity by his exquisite word sense and delightfully apt imagery.... His work is a fresh contribution to modern poetry as a whole." His *Poesía, 1915–56* (Universidad de Puerto Rico, 1957) reveals his more personal side as a lyric poet, ill at ease in the world.

"Prelude in Boricua": Published in *American Prefaces* (Winter 1942) and in CPII. From Palés Matos's *Tuntún de pasa y grifería: poemas afroantillanos* (Biblioteca de Autores Puertorriqueños, 1937; *Tom-Toms of Kinky Hair and All Things Black* [Universidad de Puerto Rico, 2010]).

In *American Prefaces*, WCW published the following "note" with the poem:

> This not-to-be-called translation of Matos's introductory poem from the collection *Tuntún de Pasa y Grifería* is offered with profound apologies to the poet [whom WCW had met in Puerto Rico, in 1941, while at the First Inter-American Writers' Conference]. It is no more than an approximate translation which makes no attempt to give the musical sense of the original. Some of the words cannot be rendered in English at all, not even in American nigger talk. The mood is West Indian, as are the words which portray the mood. *Poemas Afroantillanos* is what Matos calls them.

Boricua is the popular local name for Puerto Rico that derives from the indigenous Taíno name for the island, *Bo-ri-ken*, appearing in Spanish as *Boriquén* or *Borinquén*; the first recorded use of this name ("Borinque") is found in Columbus's "Letter to the Sovereigns" (4 Mar. 1493).

Julio Marzán emphasizes that the name has broader implications, especially in the context of the poem here:

> The "Boricua" in the Palés Matos title is not a reference to Borinquén but to the island's colloquial idiom. The standard criticism on PM had no idea what he was doing (not just in this poem but in all his work; nobody grasped the complexity and depth of this great poet) and came up with his having applied *boricua* as a variant of P.R. A *boricua*, or someone from P.R., speaks *boricua*. WCW's

fascination with PM's *Tuntún* was its being in his (W's) baroque Spanish line and written in an American idiom, i.e., PM's doing exactly what he was doing. (E)

In Marzán's critical work *The Numinous Site: The Poetry of Luis Palés Matos* (Fairleigh Dickinson University Press, 1995), he comments on WCW's response to the poem: "While Palés's near-Gongorine style and Williams's apparent free-flowing verse may seem incompatible, Williams immediately grasped that Palés had written a poetry that uses local talk and humor with utmost seriousness." And in his book *The Spanish American Roots of William Carlos Williams* (University of Texas Press, 1994), he argues that WCW's free verse encoded a baroque imagination influenced by Góngora.

"Trip" for *mondongo* (tripe) in the last line of the second stanza is possibly a typo, or an attempt by WCW to represent African-American speech. Mondongo, tripe stew, is a popular Puerto Rican dish, like funche (boiled cornmeal) that appears in the same line.

ANONYMOUS NAHUATL POETS; Mexico. The authors of the ninety-one songs, or poems, in the sixteenth-century manuscript known as *Cantares mexicanos* ("Mexican Songs")—recognized as the chief source of Aztec poetry—were not literary figures in the modern sense. Most of the songs in this codex were composed during the immediate post-Conquest period, but surely have roots in the much older oral tradition and, as some scholars believe, likely derive from songs by kings and other nobility. Indeed, they belong to the tradition of the first poets in the Americas.

"Three Nahuatl Poems": Published in WCW's *Pictures from Brueghel* (New Directions, 1962) and in CPII. First published in *The Muse in Mexico: A Mid-Century Miscellany* (University of Texas Press, 1959). From *Historia de la literatura náhuatl* (Porrúa, 1953; "History of Nahuatl Literature"), by Angel María Garibay (1892–1967). JVA provided the Spanish texts, along with his literal translations.

The verses forming this sequence are fragments of songs from the *Cantares mexicanos*, and are based on the Spanish rendering of them by Garibay, a scholar of pre-Columbian Mesoamerican cultures, specifically of the Nahua peoples of the central Mexican highlands. WCW made his translations at the request of JVA, who sent him the three "poems," which he had culled from Garibay's *Historia de la literatura náhuatl*. The translated poems were to appear in ER, as part of the planned special feature on Mexican writing, but they did not, perhaps because of the decision to focus on contemporary works.

The discrepancy in the opening line of the third poem between "el príncipe, el Aguila Cacamatl" in the Spanish and "prince Cuautli" in the translation may derive from JVA's intervention, as *águila* means "eagle" in Spanish and *cuautli* means "eagle" in Nahuatl. Cacamatl was the name of two or more pre-Conquest kings, as well as the name of a nephew of Montezuma II, the ruler of Texcoco and a resistance hero killed by the Spaniards in 1520.

OCTAVIO PAZ; Mexico, 1914–1998. Poet, diplomat, essayist, cultural historian, professor. His first book of poetry came out in 1933. Neruda helped him to travel to Spain during the Civil War, where he met the best Spanish poets. After a phase of writing political poems, he moved to Paris, and entered a surrealistic phase, which ended in the mid-1950s with the publication of *Sunstone*, one of the century's great poetic achievements. Mexico's foremost man of letters, he helped to define modern poetry and the Mexican personality. He won the Nobel Prize in 1990.

"Hymn Among the Ruins": Published in Paz's *Early Poems, 1935–1955* (New Directions, 1973). This edition was edited by Muriel Rukeyser, an expanded and revised version of her 1963 collection published by Indiana University Press. The 1963 edition contained her translation, not WCW's. His original also in CPII. The version here published in Paz's *Selected Poems* (New Directions, 1984), edited by Eliot Weinberger; see details below.

From Paz's *Libertad bajo palabra* (Tezontle, 1949; "Freedom on Parole"); dated 1948.

In the *London Magazine* (June/July 1974), Paz describes his response to WCW's translation: "In 1955, if I remember correctly [1958, actually], Donald Allen sent me a translation into English of a poem of mine, 'Hymn Among the Ruins.' The translation made a double impression on me: it was a magnificent translation and the translator was William Carlos Williams. I promised myself a meeting with him." (The two later met in Rutherford, and Paz says: "I have never met a man less affected. Just the opposite of an oracle. Possessed by poetry, not by his role as a poet.") Describing his own translation poetics, Paz comments that "literalness is not only impossible, it's reprehensible."

WCW made his translation at the request of Donald Allen, editor of *Evergreen Review*, who provided the Spanish text along with a recent "plain prose" translation of it by J. M. Cohen. Allen had hoped to include WCW's rendering in verse in the Mexican feature of ER, telling him in a letter that Paz was "very 'entusiasmado con la idea de que William Carlos Williams traduzca [excited about the idea that WCW would translate] el *Himno entre Ruinas*'" (YALE). However, two other poems by Paz were included instead.

Cohen's translation had appeared in his 1956 anthology, *The Penguin Book of Spanish Verse*. Here is his prose rendering of the first stanza, for comparison with WCW's work:

> Crowned with itself, the day displays its plumage. Tall yellow shout, hot geyser in the middle of an impartial and beneficent sky! Appearances are beautiful in this, their transient truth. The sea mounts the coast, clings between the rocks, a dazzling spider; the livid wound on the mountain glistens; a handful of goats is a flock of stones; the sun lays its golden egg and spills upon the sea. All is god. A broken statue, columns gnawed by the light, living ruins in a world of living dead.

In the first publication of WCW's translation in Paz's *Early Po-ems*, the following three lines critical of Western capitalism do not appear: "*Domestic bipeds, their flesh— / despite recent reli-gious prohibitions— / is much-loved by the wealthy classes.*" However, they do appear in the version in Paz's 1984 *Selected Poems*, as well as in the present collection. They were added by Weinberger, who translated them, to be consistent with the com-plete poem in Spanish (E).

WCW had omitted these lines probably to avoid a repeat of the political nightmare he endured in 1952. Public accusations against him for being a communist sympathizer had blocked his appointment as consultant in poetry at the Library of Congress. He felt the burden of that situation had seriously jeopardized his post-stroke physical health. When he made his translation in the late 1950s, McCarthyism was still a potent force.

The literal translation of the poem's famous last line, "palabras que son flores que son frutos que son actos," is "words that are flowers that are fruits that are acts." WCW's rendering of this line, which does not conform to the literal, transforms it in a dis-tinctive manner.

PABLO NERUDA; Chile, 1904–1973. Poet, diplomat, politi-cian. The book of love poems he published at twenty was a sen-sation. He served all over the world in the consular service from 1927 on. Living in Spain during the mid-1930s, he became a close friend of Lorca and other leading Spanish poets. His image-driven surrealist poetics, in particular that of his *Residencia en la tierra* (Árbol, 1935; *Residence on Earth* [New Directions, 1973]), had a marked influence on U.S. poetry during the 1960s and '70s. The most famous Latin American poet of the twentieth century, he won the Nobel Prize in 1971.

"Ode to Laziness": Published in CPII. First published in NWW. From *Odas elementales* (Losada, 1954; "Elemental Odes").

Translation requested by JVA, who provided his literal translation (YALE).

John Felstiner observes that in this translation WCW is "translating quite closely while still moving to his own deft measure" (*Translating Neruda* [Stanford University Press, 1980]).

WCW's first-person rendering of the verb *debía* (line 3), which can be read as either "I ought" or "it ought," differs from that of other translators of this poem (e.g., W. S. Merwin, Stephen Mitchell, Margaret Sayers Peden), who use the third person. WCW follows JVA's translation of this line to the letter.

"Ode to My Socks": Typescript at YALE. First published in HR. From *Nuevas odas elementales* (Losada, 1956; "New Elemental Odes"). Translation requested by JVA for publication in NWW, which did not occur. JVA provided the Spanish text, along with his literal translation (YALE).

"Maru Mori" (line 1) was the wife of the distinguished Chilean painter Camilo Mori, and a friend of the poet.

WCW's translations of both odes demonstrate one of the things he liked so much about Neruda's poetry, how—as he says in his 1960 poem "Tribute to Neruda the Poet Collector of Seashells"— the "changeless beauty of / seashells, like the / sea itself, gave / his lines the variable pitch / which modern verse requires" (CPII).

ALÍ CHUMACERO; Mexico, 1918–2010. Poet, essayist, editor. His first book of poetry, *Páramo de sueños* (Universidad Nacional Autónoma de México, 1944; "Wilderness of Dreams"), won a major prize and critical acclaim. He was founding editor of the bimonthly literary journal *Tierra Nueva* (1940–1942), and for several years he was director of Fondo de Cultura Económica, one of Mexico's most prestigious publishing houses. His poems often explore the themes of solitude, time, and death. His work exerted a significant influence on the development of contemporary Mexican poetry.

"Green Eyes": Published in CPII. First published in NWW. From Chumacero's *Palabras en reposo* (Fondo de Cultura Económica, 1956; "Words at Rest"). The translation of this poem, as with the other two Chumacero poems here, was made at the request of JVA, who provided WCW with the Spanish texts, along with his literal translations (YALE).

"Widower's Monologue": Published in CPII. First published in ER. From Chumacero's *Palabras en reposo*. JVA told WCW in a letter: "[This] is a poem that starts where others normally end. Here the action is all *after* the husband has buried his wife and returns to an empty house" (28 May 1958; YALE).

"The Wanderings of the Tribe": Published in CPII. First published in ER. From Chumacero's *Palabras en reposo*. JVA told WCW in a letter: "[This] is an attempt to tell the whole story of the conquest of Mexico by the Spaniards" (28 May 1958; YALE).

NICANOR PARRA; Chile, 1914– . Poet, scientist, professor. From 1952 to his retirement in 1991 he taught theoretical physics. His first book of poetry, *Cancionero sin nombre* (Nascimento, 1937; "Songbook without a Name"), presaged his use in later "antipoetry"—a free verse opposed to established poetics— of colloquial, often irreverent language and humor. With *Poemas y antipoemas* (Nascimento, 1954; *Poems and Antipoems* [New Directions, 1967]), his efforts to make poetry more accessible made him famous in Chile and throughout the world. He is considered one of the most important Latin American poets.

"Piano Solo": Published in Parra's *Poems and Antipoems* and in CPII. First published in NWW; translation made at the request of JVA. From Parra's *Poemas y antipoemas*. JVA also provided his literal translation (YALE).

ÁLVARO FIGUEREDO; Uruguay, 1907–1966. Poet, essayist, educator. During his lifetime, he published two books of poetry, *Desvío de la estrella* (Talleres La Paz, 1936; "Detour by the Star") and *Mundo a la vez* (Rosgal, 1956; "World at Once"). The same year he published his first book he founded the monthly literary magazine, *Mástil*. His work has only recently begun to be more widely studied internationally. He is regarded as one of the main poets of Uruguay, and in his birthplace Pan de Azúcar, a cultural center and museum and the town's high school bear his name.

"Naked": Published in CPII. First published in NWW; translation made at the request of JVA, who provided his literal translation (YALE). From *Mundo a la vez*. Álvaro Tell Figueredo, the poet's son, relates: "My father was quite satisfied by that work by an American poet" (E).

SILVINA OCAMPO; Argentina, 1903–1993. Poet, artist, short-story writer, translator. Her first books of poetry, published in the early 1940s, won acclaim throughout Latin America. The magic realism of her prose, marked by the coexistence of cruelty and innocence, tests the limits of what people think they know about the world. She translated Dickinson, Poe, and Melville. She was a lifelong friend of Borges, who once said she was "one of the best poets in Spanish." ACLAP notes: "Hers is one of the most moving voices in contemporary American poetry."

"The Infinite Horses": Published in CPII. First published in NWW; translation made at the request of JVA. From Ocampos's *Espacios métricos* (Sur, 1945; "Metrical Spaces"). JVA also provided his literal translation (YALE).

WCW's rendering of *temían* (line 10; lit. "feared") as "keep" is based on JVA's translation of the line as "had them under the palms of their hands."

The *tarpanes* in the Spanish text (line 22) are horses, specifically, the extinct subspecies of wild horse called tarpan, also known as the Eurasian wild horse (the last one died in captivity in Russia in 1909).

Suzanne Jill Levine tells this anecdote about WCW and Ocampo: "He wrote to her, asking permission to translate a poem of hers: she never wrote back, thinking he was a Brazilian musician" (E).

ERNESTO MEJÍA SÁNCHEZ; Nicaragua, 1923–1985. Poet, diplomat, essayist, professor. He was one of the leading poets of the so-called 1940s Generation in Nicaragua, along with Ernesto Cardenal. His first book, *Ensalmos y conjuros* (Cuadernos Americanos, 1947; "Spells and Incantations"), displayed a brilliant poetic style of brevity and precision. Steven White says: "Solitude, purification, angels, and fiends are some of the themes that haunt his poetry." Much of his work conveys a moralistic tone that expresses his political convictions and sense of justice. He left Nicaragua for Mexico.

"Vigils": Typescript at YALE. First published in *Words Without Borders: The Online Magazine for International Literature* (July 2011). From Mejía Sánchez's *Contemplaciones europeas* (Ministerio de Cultura, 1957; "European Contemplations"). Translation requested by JVA for publication in NWW, which did not occur. JVA provided the Spanish text and his literal translation (YALE).

JORGE CARRERA ANDRADE; Ecuador, 1902–1978. Poet, journalist, diplomat, professor. He published his first book of poetry in 1926. He centered his mature poetry on the metaphor as his basic unit of composition. During the 1920s and '30s he lived in Germany, Spain, and France. In 1938 he was in Japan, where he experimented with the *haiku* form, publishing a small book of poems in this medium, titled *Microgramas* (Asia América, 1940; *Micrograms* [Wave Books, 2011]). He then served as consul in San Francisco. In 1946, his *Secret Country*, translated by Muna Lee, was much celebrated in the United States.

In a letter, WCW thanked Lee for introducing him to Carrera Andrade's poetry (6 July 1942): "I don't know when I have had so clear a pleasure, so unaffected by the torments of mind which are today our daily bread. The images are as you say so extraordinarily clear, so related to the primitive that I think I am seeing as an aborigine saw and sharing that lost view of the world. It's a sad pleasure but a great one." ACLAP notes: "The fresh immediacy of this verse, together with its extraordinary invention and sharp wit, makes it a signal contribution to American literature."

"Dictated by the Water": Typescript at YALE. From Carrera Andrade's *Familia de la noche* (Librería Española de Ediciones, 1953; "Family of Night"). Translation requested by JVA for publication in NWW, which did not occur. JVA provided the Spanish text, along with his literal translation (YALE). First published in Jonathan Cohen's "Into the American Idiom: William Carlos Williams's Translation of Jorge Carrera Andrade's 'Dictado por el agua,'" *Translation Review* 77/78 (2009).

The Spanish text used for the translation is from the 1953 edition of *Familia de la noche*, which contains a typographical error—or, perhaps, deliberate early word choice—in line 13: the word *cabello* (hair) in subsequent collections of Carrera Andrade's work is instead *caballo* (horse).

EUGENIO FLORIT; Cuba, 1903–1999. Poet, diplomat, essayist, professor. He spent his early years in Spain; his father was Spanish, his mother Cuban. At fifteen he moved to Cuba. His first book, *32 poemas breves* (Hermes, 1927; "32 Short Poems"), was published there. In 1940, he came to New York to work for the Cuban consulate, and started teaching Hispanic literature at Barnard. One of Cuba's most influential poets, he sought the essence of poetic language. TSAP notes: "There are few Spanish

American poets who can be compared with Florit for graceful artistry."

"Conversation with My Father": Typescript at YALE. First published in HR. From Florit's *Conversación a mi padre* (Ayón, 1949; "Conversation with My Father"); poem dated 3 Nov. 1948. Translation requested by JVA for publication in NWW, which did not occur. JVA also provided his literal translation (YALE).

The typescript of WCW's translation contains the following passage toward the poem's end in which he apparently confuses the meaning of *temple* (tempera) with *templo* (temple): "and those blue skies that you painted in tempera / for the Nativity scenes *that you used to paint for the temple / of the Nativity* you made for us in Port-Bou." The faulty section, shown here in italics, has been deleted from the translation in the present collection. JVA's rendering, which WCW used together with the Spanish, follows: "and those blue skies that you painted in tempera / for the Nativity scenes which you use [*sic*] to make for us at Port-Bou."

Las Meninas ("Maids of Honor") is a 1656 painting by Diego Velázquez, the leading artist of the Spanish Golden Age, housed in the Museo del Prado in Madrid. The work's complex composition raises questions about reality and illusion.

La Duquesa de Alba ("The Duchess of Alba") is the main title of two paintings by Francisco Goya (1746–1828), the Spanish Romantic painter and printmaker regarded both as the last of the Old Masters and the first of the moderns: "The Duchess of Alba in White" and "The Duchess of Alba in Black." The subject of these paintings is Cayetana de Silva, 13th Duchess of Alba.

At the time Florit wrote this poem, Cayetana Fitz-James Stuart y Silva, 18th Duchess of Alba, was (and still is) an international celebrity aristocrat.

RAQUEL HÉLÈNE (ELENA) ROSE HOHEB WILLIAMS; Puerto Rico, 1847–1950. Would-be artist, Francophile, homemaker, mother of WCW. She was half French, and studied art in Paris at the Académie des Beaux-Arts in the late 1870s. WCW told Louis Untermeyer in a letter (5 Mar. 1941): "Her mother was born in Martinique, her name was Meline Hurrard (a Basque name as all names ending in -ard should be), her father's name was Solomon Hoheb who was born in St Thomas. His ancestry was Dutch-Jewish-Spanish so far as I can learn" (BLOOMINGTON).

"From My Window." Published in both Spanish and English in WCW's "personal record" of his mother, *Yes, Mrs. Williams* (New Directions, 1959). WCW notes: "Her only poem!"

When WCW's mother was an art student in Paris, she lived with her French cousins Alice and Ludovic Monsanto. Through the Monsanto side of his mother's family, WCW was related to Lawrence Ferlinghetti, who explains: "Yes, indeed, my uncle, Ludovic Monsanto [with whom the quasi-orphaned Ferlinghetti lived as a youngster, in Brooklyn], was the same Monsanto who was the cousin of W. C. Williams's mother, and I have a snapshot of my Aunt Gladys in St. Thomas posing with WC and Flossy. WC and I thought that the relation with Ludovic was a wonderful coincidence. (My mother's name was Clemence Albertine Monsanto.)" (E)

WCW says about his mother in *Yes, Mrs. Williams*: "She was no more than an obscure art student from Puerto Rico, slaving away at her trade which she loved with her whole passionate soul, living it, drinking it down with her every breath—the money gone, her mother as well as her father now dead, she was forced to return with her scanty laurels, a Grand Prix, a few gold medals to disappear into a trunk in my attic, a few charcoal sketches, a full length portrait of herself, unfinished, by that Ludovic, showing her ungainly hands. From Paris she returned to these meager islands

[West Indies]. She married at the home of one of those same Monsantos and pretty soon had two boys on her hands."

Elena's brother, Carlos Benjamin Hoheb Hurrard (1845–1898), a surgeon, after whom WCW was named, introduced her to his best friend, WGW. Their father, Solomon Hoheb, was the son of Samuel Hoheb, the first in their family to come to America from Holland—to Sint Eustatius, Netherlands Antilles—in the late 1700s; the elder Hoheb was the son of Samuel Hoheb Lopes, whose family roots went back to Spain before the Inquisition.

EUNICE ODIO; Costa Rica, 1922–1974. Poet, journalist. She lived in several Central American countries. In 1959, she moved to New York, where she spent two and a half years. She infused her poetry with Christian mysticism; she imagined she had personal relations with the archangel Michael. JVA described her work as "celestially metaphysical poetry," and said her masterpiece "Fire's Journey"—a sequence of some 10,000 lines—was "unquestionably Middle America's most powerful bid for the crown in Spanish poetry since the legendary days of Sor Juana."

"To W.C.W.": Typescript at YALE. First published in *The New Yorker* (4 Oct. 2010). Not included in Odio's published work. WCW's "free" translation (imitation) of Odio's poem is based on her Spanish as well as the literal translation of it made by JVA (YALE), titled "To the Poet William Carlos Williams," which follows:

> In him was contained
> the arbor.
>
> It was his will,
>
> an entrance
> to the clear designs
> of waters.

The sounds of heaven
were heard with his hearing.

(When God made a sound
not tasted by the moon,
nor cleared by the wind,

he thought it was the coming
of daybreak's rumors,

and it was that he heard the silence
of God become still.)

When I saw him
by afternoon surrounded,

—island face,
longitude of air—,

when I came up to him
from within myself,

the infant tassel of wheat
poured out its heart:

gave it to April's water,
to the shade of May,
to the burning passing of the summer.

The nightingale reclining
dreamt of laurel,

and the laurel
of the transparent hart.

And the world which was an eye
shut to the cadence
of the wing, the stone, the torrent,

opened, gazed upon its shape,
loved its living image thence forever.

Saw that it was good
because in it was held
the boundaries of flight.

Odio's poem was written after her visit, with JVA, to WCW's home in September 1959. In her letter she sent to him with the poem, she told him that only poetry could express how deeply moving the experience of their meeting him had been for her. She wrote: "En su casa me sentí, por primera vez en mucho tiempo, frente al poeta verdadero, hecho de materias bondadosas, por el cual el mundo se justifica y conoce a sí mismo" [In your home I felt I was, for the first time in a long time, facing a true poet, made of the very stuff of kindness, who enables the world to prove and know itself]. And she offered her poem as a tribute in thanks.

Among WCW's deviations from the literal meaning of the poem is his rendering of the word *ciervo* (stag) as "heart."

Acknowledgments

Grateful acknowledgment—for access to the papers of William Carlos Williams—is made to Breon Mitchell, Lilly Library, Indiana University Bloomington, with special gratitude to the Lilly Library for the Everett Helm Visiting Fellowship; Molly Wheeler and Eva Guggemos, Beinecke Rare Book and Manuscript Library, Yale University; and James Maynard, Poetry Collection, University at Buffalo. Further acknowledgments are due Lea Cline, Harry Ransom Center, University of Texas at Austin, and Melissa Gasparotto, Archibald S. Alexander Library, Rutgers University; Williams scholars and aficionados Paul Mariani, Christopher MacGowan, Emily Mitchell Wallace, Neil Baldwin, Bill Zavatsky, Natalie Gerber, and Gabriele Hayden; Charles Hatfield, *Translation Review*, for publishing "Dictated by the Water"; Paul Muldoon, *The New Yorker*, for publishing "To W.C.W."; Susan Harris, *Words Without Borders*, for publishing "Vigils"; Paula Deitz, *The Hudson Review*, for publishing "Conversation with My Father" and "Ode to My Socks"; Julio Marzán for his illumination and his essential foreword; New Directions' entire team for this book, with extra thanks to Declan Spring; Edith Grossman for all her encouragement and critical wisdom; other friends and colleagues, Daniel Deutsch, David Unger, Graham Everett, Ernesto Cardenal, Marjorie Agosín, Gerald Nelson, Lawrence Ferlinghetti, Jaime Manrique, Julio Ramos, Lía Schwartz de Lerner, Daniel Shapiro, Juan Zaro, Suzanne Churchill, Jacinta Amaral, Peggy von Mayer, Suzanne Jill Levine, Eliot Weinberger; and my wife, Ellen Lerner, for loving support beyond measure.

JONATHAN COHEN

Index of Titles and First Lines

About Cohen and Marzán

JONATHAN COHEN is an award-winning translator of Latin American poetry and scholar of inter-American literature. He edited the New Directions anthology of Ernesto Cardenal's poetry, *Pluriverse: New and Selected Poems.* Scholarly works include *A Pan-American Life: Selected Poetry and Prose of Muna Lee* and *Neruda in English: A Critical History of the Verse Translations and Their Impact on American Poetry.*

   See jonathancohenweb.com.

JULIO MARZÁN, former Poet Laureate of Queens, NY, is the author of *The Spanish American Roots of William Carlos Williams.* His poetry books include *Translations Without Originals* and *Puerta de tierra* ("Port of Call"). Other works are *The Numinous Site: The Poetry of Luis Palés Matos, The Bonjour Gene: A Novel,* and *Luna, Luna: Creative Writing Ideas from Spanish, Latin American, and Latino Literature.*

   See juliomarzan.com.

Also by William Carlos Williams

AVAILABLE FROM NEW DIRECTIONS

FORTHCOMING